IMAGES
of America

NEWTON

IMAGES
of *America*

NEWTON

Dena Bisnette and Joe Gilliam

ARCADIA
PUBLISHING

Published by Arcadia Publishing
Charleston, South Carolina

Library of Congress Control Number: 2012954034

For all general information, please contact Arcadia Publishing:
Telephone 843-853-2070
Fax 843-853-0044
E-mail sales@arcadiapublishing.com
For customer service and orders:
Toll-Free 1-888-313-2665

Visit us on the Internet at www.arcadiapublishing.com

*To my late father, John Eddie Bisnette, who loved history, no
matter whose it was; and to my mother, Dorothy Haidinger
Bisnette, who tolerated that history even when it bored her.*

CONTENTS

ACKNOWLEDGMENTS

We want to thank everyone who contributed images to this book. They include Helen Collins, Dr. Gil Michel, Loyette Polhans Olson and Beverley Buller, John Wiebe, Mary Schroeder of the Thelma Weston Estate, Todd Hanchett, Karen and Jerry Jacobson, Karen and Jerry Wall, Dan Hollingshead and Patti Little Hollingshead, Ron and Elaine Saunders, Glenn and Mary Lou Patrick, Phil Anderson, Val and Maurice Hind, Sharon Koehn and Arlo Kasper, Randy Regier, Zona Galle, Monica Supernois, Catherine French, Harry Kasitz, Mary Hanke, Diane Claassen, Albert Monares, Bethany Mace and Rosie Wiebe, Brad Anderson, Charlie and Mary Smith, and representatives of so many of Newton's churches that we are afraid we might leave someone out, so we will just thank them all.

We also thank Warkentin House Museum, Harvey County Historical Museum and Archive, Mennonite Library and Archives, Halstead Depot Museum, Newton Public Library, Bethel College, Mennonite Press, *Newton Kansan*, Pages, and Metcalf Sisters Antiques. Our thanks go to Prairie Harvest, The Breadbasket, Karen's Kitchen, and Taste of New Orleans for letting us tie up their tables during interviews and brainstorming sessions.

For additional information, we thank Helen Collins, John Wiebe, Karen Jacobson, Glenn Patrick, Beverley Buller; Gil Michel, Karen Penner, Keith Sprunger, John Thiesen, Zona and Omer Galle, Jim Wimmer, Rhonda Brown, Linda Koppes, and the late Mike Hurley. Thanks go to Dennis Lammers for his skill with film, Jennifer Mueller of Newton Convention and Visitors Bureau, Chad Frey at *Newton Kansan* and the folks at Pages for publicity. Also, we thank Billi Jo Wilson, members of Newton–North Newton Historic Preservation Commission, Lois Ruble, Mary and Charlie Smith, and Steve and Lorraine Richards for connections and encouragement. We also want to thank all those individuals who provided us with tips and referrals.

Finally, Dena thanks Joe for being a technical genius and scanning master, doing all of those computer things she had no idea how to do, and for doing extra duty looking after Belle, Jake, and George when she got too busy to walk them. Joe thanks Dena for helping him discover something that he now loves: trains.

INTRODUCTION

Newton, Kansas, literally arrived on a train.

In 1870, officials of the Atchison, Topeka & Santa Fe Railroad wanted to move the railhead for the Chisholm Trail, one of several routes cowboys used to bring cattle from Texas to the railroad, which would then ship the livestock to Eastern markets. A good water supply was the key to a good location, and Sand Creek supplied that.

The first days of Newton were filled with railroad construction, which, back then, was actually more important than the town; Newton itself simply grew up to support the railroad and accompanying stockyards. On an average day, most of the population was transient, consisting of cowboys and railroad workers. Newton saw its share of trouble when cowboys got their pay and got rowdy, and the sensationalism that passed for news in the early 1870s exaggerated the town's bad reputation.

Two years later, the cowboys and the disreputable characters who followed them left when the railhead moved. Newton might have dried up if it had not been for a Ukrainian immigrant named Bernhard Warkentin, a miller who turned out to be the lead scout for thousands of Mennonite farmers fleeing religious persecution in Eastern Europe. He brought Turkey Red hard winter wheat, and much needed farmers, to Kansas. The railroad, which owned all the land in and around Newton, was only too happy to invite the immigrants to Kansas and to sell them land at what they called "reasonable prices." Committees were formed to meet immigrants when they arrived in Kansas and convince them to move to Newton instead of some other town. The railroad even provided an immigrant house, temporary communal living quarters where newcomers could stay until they were able to set up their own homes.

Now the railroad had wheat to ship out, and passengers to ship in. Santa Fe operations expanded. Engine maintenance shops and yards, a roundhouse, rail mills, track maintenance equipment, and all kinds of related Santa Fe enterprises required more workers. Irishmen, Italians, Greeks, Mexicans, and African Americans came to fill the vacancies. The railroad established a division point in Newton, but when the good water supply was not so good anymore, moved it to Nickerson. Newton residents fought back, developing a brand new waterworks, offering free residential lots to Santa Fe workers, and providing years of free water for the steam-operated railroad. Santa Fe was pleased and moved back.

In the meantime, Fred Harvey moved in and started an empire. His first Harvey House restaurant may not have been in Newton, but all his support businesses were. During the late 19th and early 20th centuries, he was second only to the Santa Fe Railroad in the number of local jobs provided.

Newton became a growing town, with churches, stores, schools, shops and services, the Harvey County Courthouse, and more. Residences sprang up in the neighborhoods around the center of town, along the tracks, and around the flour mills. An African American business district flourished. The railroad provided housing for its Mexican workers.

Increased railroad traffic kept Newton going, even during the Great Depression. Newton took a hit like other places, but older residents remember that it was not as bad. World War II kept Newton busy with troop trains and freights carrying war materiel, and its proximity to Wichita meant there were plenty of airplane manufacturing jobs for those who could not find work in town. The town's position at the crossroads of Highways 81 and 50 meant that more people came through as America embraced the automobile culture.

Newton's economy began to slow down in the 1960s, as the interstate highway system took people off the trains. Newton became a manufacturing center for mobile homes, but that industry, too, faded. Chain businesses began to replace family-owned ones, some of which went back generations. People began to move away from the old part of town.

Gradually, like a plant that loses its leaves in autumn and sprouts new buds in spring, Newton began to revive. People from nearby Wichita got tired of living in the biggest city in Kansas, and, though they still worked there, many moved to Newton. Empty storefronts downtown began to fill with new businesses, such as antique shops and art galleries. Tiny starter industries again began to move into unassuming buildings in the Meridian Road area and around Newton Airport, and some of them succeeded and stayed. Newton was selected for a new logistics park, mostly due to the presence of the Burlington Northern Santa Fe Railroad.

The authors moved to Newton almost 10 years ago when Joe's job based him in Wichita. One of the first things Dena did upon their arrival was what she did every time she moved to a new town. She went for a walk.

She saw empty storefronts downtown, buildings that had seen better days, and empty houses in the neighborhood they were considering as their new home. But, she also saw something she liked: people sitting on front porches, people walking with children and dogs, and people stopping to speak to each other. Downtown, she saw the first signs of Newton's spring. An old carriage factory had been restored as an art gallery, an old mill housed offices, a store was being painted, and someone was moving into a vacant building.

In the years that followed, Dena joined the Newton/North Newton Historic Preservation Commission and volunteered at a couple of area museums. Her interest in preserving the past seemed to parallel Newton's, as she watched downtown revive and many residents improve their houses. She and Joe continue a hobby of traveling, and she finds herself mentally comparing Newton's progress to other Midwestern towns of the same size. In her opinion, spring has indeed come to Newton. The town's progress is comparable to that of others and surpasses many, despite negative national economic statistics. Summer, that most desirable season, may still seem a long way off, but Newton is definitely looking ahead to it.

Dena and Joe decided to stay in this town called Newton, the Crossroads of Kansas and America. They invite you to visit Newton's past in the following pages.

One

EARLY DAYS AND
MEMORABLE EVENTS

Early Newton bore an exaggerated reputation for danger, as many Old West cow towns did. Contemporary accounts often called it the "wildest, bloodiest cow town in the West."

Before the Atchison, Topeka & Santa Fe Railroad was completed, cowboys driving cattle up the Chisholm Trail from Texas passed through town en route to Abilene. But when Newton became the shipping point, they stopped in town. As Judge R.W.P. Muse recorded, "About the first of June [1871], in anticipation of the cattle trade, the festive cowboy, gamblers, saloon men, and roughs of every description began to flock in." Soon, dance halls and saloons, attracting gamblers, prostitutes, pickpockets, and trouble, followed. The first passenger train in Newton arrived on July 17, 1871, bringing more people to support the cattle trade. A few were actually respectable citizens, but they are not the ones people usually tell stories about.

Most of Newton's bad reputation can be traced to the "general massacre" on August 9, 1871, when a cowboy named Jim Anderson shot a man named McCloskey in Perry Tuttle's saloon. Before dying, McCloskey shot and crippled Anderson. A young man named Riley, seeing his friend McCloskey fall, quietly locked the door and opened fire, killing two men and wounding others.

More incidents brought the number of shooting murders in Newton's cow town era to perhaps 12, instead of 40 or 50, as rumored. The exact number is hard to determine, lost between legend and truth. There was enough excitement, however, that a section near the present downtown was nicknamed Hide Park, a useful instruction when cowboys mixed liquor with guns.

The railhead moved again two years later. The cowboys left, and Newton became respectable. Immigrants, especially Mennonite farmers, arrived, and a new chapter of Newton's history began.

A wagon crosses Sand Creek south of the Tenth Street Bridge. The Chisholm Trail crossed the creek west of the bridge, where the bottom was rock instead of mud. Cowboys driving cattle, stagecoaches, supply wagons, and other travelers crossed there from 1867 to 1871 en route to Abilene. According to one estimate, 600,000 cattle crossed annually. Local legend has it that marks left by hooves and wheels may be seen on the creek bottom in times of extreme drought. (Courtesy Dr. Gil Michel.)

Another Sand Creek scene resembles what Judge R.W.P. Muse and D.L. Lakin, land department commissioner of the Atchison, Topeka & Santa Fe Railroad, and their party found in August 1870 while searching for a suitable site for a new town and railhead for the Chisholm Trail. They left Topeka by train on August 24 for Emporia, then terminus of the line, and continued by wagon with stops in Cottonwood Falls and at a ranch near the present-day town of Peabody. They then passed through what became Walton and arrived at Sand Creek on August 28. Muse, writing 10 years later, said they looked at two sections of land and, "liking the country," selected Section 19. They called the town Newton after Newton, Massachusetts, the hometown of several railroad officials. According to Muse, the new town had "perhaps 500 settlers" by October 1, 1871. The new Harvey County, named for an ex-governor of Kansas, was organized by legislative act on February 29, 1872, and Newton, despite allegations of vote tampering, was chosen as the county seat. (Courtesy Loyette Polhans Olson and Beverley Buller.)

A photographer named Tripp recorded this scene in 1872, the year Newton officially became a town. On the right is a saloon. At left is A.F. Hoerner Storage and Supply, a structure dragged in from Florence to win a cash prize for first building. The town well, dug by Capt. David Payne, was in the middle of Main Street. The railroad tracks are the photograph's most important feature, because cattle driven up the Chisholm Trail from Texas were loaded in Newton for shipment. The railhead continuously moved, so Newton's cow town era lasted only two years. Several fatal shootings contributed to Newton's reputation as "the bloodiest cow town in the west." (Courtesy Gil Michel.)

One primary feature of Newton's Main Street in 1880 was Peter Luhn's Pioneer Store, seen at right in this photograph. History records the store as one of the first three businesses in Newton, along with a bakery and a blacksmith. Luhn's store was probably the town's first permanent building and stood where Midland Bank stands today. In 1977, when the bank underwent extensive renovations, workers uncovered a limestone wall from Luhn's store. The wall was incorporated into the bank's interior design. (Courtesy John Wiebe.)

Bernhard Warkentin, a Mennonite from Ukraine, came to Kansas about 1870 looking for farmland to grow Turkey Red hard winter wheat. While studying English and milling in Illinois, he met Wilhelmina Eisenmayer, and they were later married. They originally settled in Halstead, but he later bought Monarch Steam Mills in Newton and organized Newton Milling Company. His 16-room Queen Anne–style home at 211 East First Street is now a museum. Warkentin became one of the most influential citizens in Newton, helping to found Bethel College, Bethel Deaconess Hospital, Kansas State Bank, Newton Commercial Club, and other business and civic organizations. He also worked with the railroad to bring in more than 5,000 Mennonite farmers to grow wheat in Kansas. (Courtesy Warkentin House Museum.)

This letter, dated December 20, 1908, bears a surprise: the writer, who signs it "Charlie and wife," had gotten married just three days before. Charles Weston worked out of Newton for the Santa Fe Railroad. "Wife" was Carrie Russell, whose father ran a Newton meat market. The letterhead belongs to one of several organizations cooperating with the Santa Fe Railroad to help immigrants settle in Kansas. Since he was not a German immigrant, Weston must have obtained the stationery through the railroad. (Courtesy Thelma Weston Estate.)

13

Bernhard Warkentin's wife, Wihelmina "Minna" Eisenmayer Warkentin, plays with her four grandchildren a few months after she was widowed. Bernhard died at age 60 on April 1, 1908, while traveling with his wife and a party of friends in the Holy Land. A young man in the next train compartment showed his traveling companions a pistol. When he pulled the trigger to show that the gun was not loaded, a bullet went through the compartment wall and wounded Bernhard, who later died at a hospital in Beirut. (Courtesy Warkentin House Museum.)

Residents could enjoy lounging outside on the open porch balconies in the 1960's.

Wilhelmina Warkentin was known for philanthropic work, including support of Bethel Deaconess Hospital and other causes. She supported construction of a home for hospital nurses as well as Bethel Deaconess Home for the Aged. When she died in 1932 at age 79, she left her own home to the nurses. The Bethel Home for the Aged, shown here, was just south of the hospital. Kidron Bethel Village in North Newton replaced the home in 1996. (Courtesy Loyette Polhans Olson and Beverley Buller.)

14

At several times in Newton's history, the town has flooded. This flood on North Main Street in 1904 was immortalized on a postcard from a souvenir folder once sold by Anderson's. (Courtesy Todd Hanchett.)

A young passerby checks the level of floodwaters during a Sand Creek flood in 1923. The dam was north of the First Street Bridge at the time. Note the homes on the other side of the creek. Other photographs in the same group showed fast-moving floodwaters. (Courtesy John Wiebe.)

Newton residents turned out on October 3, 1908, to hear Republican presidential candidate William Howard Taft speak from the rear platform of a train. US senator Charles Curtis accompanied Taft. In 1900, Pres. Theodore Roosevelt had also stopped to make a speech during his campaign. (Courtesy Todd Hanchett.)

John C. Nicholson, a lawyer and one of Newton's pioneer citizens, stands on a car's running board at Main Street and Broadway. In 1910, Nicholson began traveling by automobile, speaking to town leaders across America about the need for better roads. He wanted to make Newton the central point on a proposed road from Canada to Mexico. Named the Meridian Highway because it followed the sixth principal meridian, the project made Newton "The Crossroads of America." The Meridian Highway, later designated US 81, intersected with US 50 at Main Street and Broadway. A later reroute moved the intersection. Nicholson lived into old age and, ironically, died from injuries received in a car accident. (Courtesy Harvey County Historical Museum and Archive.)

The First Interurban Cars, Newton, Kans.   Oct. 11, 1911.

Newton residents watch the first Arkansas Valley Interurban cars go through town on October 11, 1911. The electricity-powered AVI took Newton commuters to Bethel College in North Newton, Burrton, Halstead, Hutchinson, Sedgewick, Van Arsdale, Valley Center, and Wichita. Automobile and bus traffic contributed to the line's decline in the 1920s. Passenger service ended in 1938. (Courtesy Todd Hanchett.)

What was then the world's largest locomotive visits Newton in 1911. It was 120 feet long, weighed 850,000 pounds, and cost $43,820. The steam-powered engine was taken on tour and may have been one of the sights at the San Francisco Exposition of 1912. (Courtesy Karen Jacobson.)

17

Ruins of the Fire, Newton Kans Aug 4, 1914

An August 4, 1914, fire started in the Newton City Auditorium on East Fifth Street and destroyed almost a full city block and most businesses within it. The Newton Fire Department stopped the flames from spreading, receiving help from the Santa Fe Railroad Fire Department. Santa Fe employees stood on train engines to spray water on buildings north of the tracks. H.S. Stovall, a Newton photographer who liked working in the panoramic format so much that he signed some of his photographs "The Panorama Man," recorded this sweeping image. The Kansas & Missouri

Telephone Company advertised in the newspaper after the tragedy, asking people to refrain from using telephones for the "curiosity calls" that flooded their switchboards and thus "lessen the danger of fires." This was the first of two major downtown fires within a few months. The second was the New Year's Eve fire that destroyed the Ragsdale Opera House; its tower shows in the background, at center. (Courtesy Jerry Wall.)

Newton City Auditorium, shown here shortly after completion in 1913, was one of several structures designed by architect Samuel Greenebaum, a Newton High graduate. Those buildings included Newton High School, built in 1914; Lincoln Elementary School (1917); Hotel Ripley and Railroad Building & Loan (both 1925); and Bethel College Alumni Hall. The demolished Newton High building lot is now part of Santa Fe School's campus. Lincoln School was modified for adaptive reuse as an apartment building for the elderly. Hotel Ripley was demolished in 1974. Railroad Building & Loan now houses the Newton Area Chamber of Commerce and several businesses. (Courtesy John Wiebe.)

CARNEGIE LIBRARY   NEWTON, KANSAS.

About 1900, philanthropist Andrew Carnegie began giving grants for construction of new public libraries. Newton received $16,000 in grants. The Carnegie library, constructed in 1904, enabled the existing city library to move from rental quarters at Fifth and Main Streets, where the Randall Building now stands. A $5,000 addition expanded the library in 1924. The basement was remodeled in 1937 to create a children's wing. The Carnegie library closed in 1973 when a new library was constructed. Today, the Carnegie library serves as museum and headquarters for the Harvey County Historical Society and is a major downtown historic landmark. (Courtesy Karen Jacobsen.)

Old Stand Pipe, Newton, Kansas.
Livingston Photo.

The replacement of the old standpipe water tower in Newton is shown in these 1908 photographs. The first, tagged "Livingston Photo," shows the old pipe with damage to its stone base. The second, published by Anderson Book Store, shows the top of the old tower being removed. (Courtesy Karen Jacobson, Phil Anderson, and Karen Jacobson.)

Now Notice Newton, Kansas. Purest Water in the State.

New Steel Water Tower 120 ft. High, holds 675,000 gallon

Newton's Mission Water 99.6/10% Pure. 1,000,000 gallons used daily

This photograph shows the new tower, which was 30 feet in diameter, 130 feet high, and cost $16,000 plus freight under a contract with Santa Fe Railroad. This tower and the tower on the previous page stood at Twelfth and Walnut Streets, where the modern tower stands today. The modern tower has been painted with a sky and clouds in the style of Newton artist Phil Epp. (Courtesy Karen Jacobson, Phil Anderson, and Karen Jacobson.)

When Newton was new, the town well was at the intersection of Main and Fifth Streets. Playing the parts of cowboys at a replica of the pump during Newton's 75th anniversary celebration in 1947 are, from left to right, Louis Earl Deschner, Eddie Godsoe, John Dickey, John Androes, Earl Henry, J. Sidney Nye, and Frank Plummer. (Courtesy Harvey County Historical Museum and Archive.)

Pres. Harry S. Truman speaks from the back of a train during his whistle-stop campaign in 1948. According to a transcript at the Harry S. Truman Library and Museum, Truman said to the crowd, "It looks like the whole city is here. I like Newton, Kansas. I have been here many a time—on business, on pleasure, and for a lot of other reasons too numerous to mention." (Photograph, Frank Little Jr.; courtesy Patti Little Hollingshead.)

President Truman reaches from the back platform of a train to shake hands with one of the people who came to hear him speak at Newton on June 16, 1948. Truman's Republican opponent, Thomas Dewey, also spoke in Newton. (Photograph, Frank Little Jr.; courtesy Pattie Little Hollingshead.)

In one of the more peculiar Kansas political stories, Newtonian John McCuish was appointed governor in 1957 to complete Fred Hall's unexpired term. McCuish served only 11 days. His only major action while in office was appointing Hall to the Kansas Supreme Court after both Hall and the chief justice resigned following Hall's unsuccessful re-election bid. McCuish was politically active in other ways, however. He served four years on the Kansas Commission on taxation, beginning in 1939, and was a delegate to the Republican National Convention in 1936 and 1948. The US Army sent him to Japan in 1950 to help establish newspapers there, and in 1952, McCuish helped direct the Kansas Eisenhower for President campaign. He died on March 12, 1957. (Courtesy Harvey County Historical Museum and Archive.)

In February 1962, Sand Creek escaped its banks. In this photograph, floodwaters threaten houses at 107 Southeast Seventh Street. A worse flood in 1965 spread water up Tenth Street to the middle of the 1300 block, Newton native Phil Anderson recalls. Another flood, in April 1974, flooded Athletic Park and extended to streets downtown. Local residents remember a small zoo in the park, where some animals were removed before the water got too high. (Courtesy Karen Wall.)

In November 1955, Santa Fe Engine No. 1880 was placed on display in Military Park. Aurora E. Walker checks the back of the truck, which belonged to Merle Davidson. The locomotive sits in front of American Flour Mill on Broadway. The Baldwin-built, Prairie-style engine remains on display. During the annual Chisholm Trail Festival and other special events, the fence around the engine is opened and the public is invited to climb aboard. Glenn Patrick, a retired engineer, still has cutaway drawings he used to tell people about the engine's inner workings. (Courtesy Harvey County Historical Museum and Archive.)

Two

"I've Been Working on the Railroad"

Santa Fe Railroad continued as the city's largest employer from 1870 into the 1950s. Santa Fe merged with Burlington Northern Railroad in 1995 to form BNSF Railway, and remains one of the largest freight railroads in the United States. Today, railroad operations are not as extensive as when Newton served as Santa Fe's Middle Division Headquarters, but BNSF still runs an engine maintenance shop.

The passenger trains that brought so many settlers to Newton are all but gone now. Passenger rail reached its peak in the 1940s, when most travelers were military men and women. On some days, as many as 45 passenger trains, mostly troop trains, came through Newton. During the 1950s, Americans began traveling more by automobile and airplane. Fewer people rode trains, but more than a dozen still came through Newton every day. Today, only two Amtrak trains visit Newton, and the station does not even have a full-time agent.

The last Santa Fe passenger train stopped in Newton on May 2, 1971. If it had run a few weeks longer, the line would have served passengers at Newton for a full 100 years.

Newton is a freight railroad town now, and its heritage is not forgotten. BNSF is still one of the top three employers. Many local residents have had railroad employees in their families for three generations. Others can recall relatives and friends who worked for the many stores, hotels, restaurants, and support businesses that would never have existed without the trains.

SANTA FE SHOPS   NEWTON, KAN.

Santa Fe maintenance shops, shown on this souvenir postcard, provided many of Newton's railroad jobs. Today, a Burlington Northern Santa Fe engine maintenance facility still operates across from the city's post office and recreation center. Trains, the rail yard, and related subjects were among Newton's most popular postcard images, as were downtown buildings, bridges, and scenes along Sand Creek. Several shops in town and Fred Harvey published their own postcards. (Courtesy Todd Hanchett.)

MISSION WATER WORKS PUMPING PLANT
AND WELLS NEAR NEWTON, KANSAS
1000,000 GALLONS OF MISSION WATER ARE USED
DAILY. ITS THE PUREST WATER IN THE STATE
99 9/10 % PURE
PUB. BY H.S. DICKEY'S POST OFFICE,
NEWS STORE

Development of Newton's new waterworks at nearby Mission was essential in luring back the Santa Fe Middle Division Headquarters, which moved to Nickerson in 1879. The headquarters returned to Newton in 1897. Shortly after opening, the pumping plant and wells near Emma Creek reportedly produced a million gallons per day with a 99 percent purity rating. As added incentive, the Newton Commercial Club, heading efforts to bring back the headquarters, offered the railroad free water for seven years and 100 building lots for Santa Fe employee residences. (Courtesy Karen Jacobson.)

28

Two railroad employees, A.H. Utz (left) and Chuck Woods, pose for a photograph on Atchison, Topeka & Santa Fe engine No. 2247. This image was found with a group of railroad photographs taken at the Sand Creek yard in Newton in the 1940s. (Courtesy Ron Saunders.)

The Santa Fe roundhouse was a prominent feature of the town until its demolition in 1955. The turntable and most nearby tracks remain as part of Burlington Northern Santa Fe's engine maintenance facility. The original roundhouse, built in 1871 soon after the railroad arrived in Newton, burned down in 1880 and was rebuilt eight years later, then expanded in 1891. When the division headquarters returned to Newton from Nickerson in 1897, native stone from the Nickerson roundhouse was used to expand the Newton roundhouse again. Over time, there were additional expansions, and the modern turntable was installed in the 1930s. (Photograph, Santa Fe Railroad; courtesy Dr. Gil Michel.)

English immigrant Fred Harvey founded his Harvey House restaurants to feed train passengers. His Newton Harvey House, established in 1883 in the Arcade Hotel, later moved to the Santa Fe depot. When he died in 1901, Harvey had expanded his Newton operations to include, at various times, a hotel, newsstands, produce operation, poultry production facility, dairy, carbonation works and bottling plant, packing plant, and steam laundry. He was once the second-largest employer in Newton after the railroad. He left the business to his son Ford. (Courtesy Helen Collins, Halstead Depot Museum.)

The first Arcade Building, near the Santa Fe tracks, included the William B. Strong Hotel, named after the railroad's president. It also housed the Santa Fe depot and a dining room. Opened in 1882, it was rebuilt in 1898 and its mansard-style facade was removed. The second version housed Newton's first Harvey House restaurant and Fred Harvey Hotel. The Arcade was demolished in 1928 to accommodate construction of the present-day depot, which is now under private ownership. (Courtesy Dr. Gil Michel.)

HARVEY HOUSE AND SANTA FE DEPOT – NEWTON, KANSAS.

The second Arcade Hotel and Santa Fe depot building was on the east side of Main Street, north of the tracks, where the present-day depot was built in 1930. Opened in 1900, after the original Arcade was razed, the hotel closed by 1926, and the building was demolished in 1929 to make room for the new Tudor Revival depot. (Courtesy Ron Saunders.)

A Murphy Studio photograph shows the 1930 depot from the track side. At left in the background and to the right are marquees that once covered passengers waiting to board. When they were removed, a few of the old marquees were used to cover the Baldwin steam engine displayed in Military Park. On the north side of the depot, a stone arch once covered an iced drinking fountain donated by the City of Newton. The arch has been moved to the corner of Main and Eighth Streets. (Courtesy Phil Anderson.)

31

Santa Fe Railroad workers get together for a group photograph in 1914. (Courtesy Thelma Weston Estate.)

Santa Fe Railroad, like many large organizations, publishes a magazine for its employees. Shown here in an edition from the second decade of the 20th century is the Newton Locomotive Force. Beneath all of those workers sits a steam-powered locomotive. (Courtesy Randy Regier.)

HOTEL RIPLEY, NEWTON, KANSAS.

The four-story Ripley Hotel, built in 1925, was primarily an overnight stopover for railroad employees. It was also known for its Mexican restaurant until 1968, when the building was purchased by Midland Bank and a drive-up bank was built in its place at 114 West Fifth Street. (Courtesy Dr. Gil Michel.)

SEIBERLING TIRES

They Come via SANTA FE

Royston
Motor Equipment Co.

PHONE 466   713 MAIN ST.
NEWTON, KANSAS

Newton business owners realized how important the Santa Fe Railroad was to the local economy. This advertising card from Royston Motor Equipment Company gave credit to the railroad for bringing one of its products, Seiberling Tires, to Newton. The crossing sign provides useful safety tips. (Courtesy Loyette Polhans Olson and Beverley Buller.)

Santa Fe Railroad personnel assemble on depot stairs facing the tracks. At far left in the second row is Charles Weston, who later died from injuries received in a train accident. His daughter Thelma told family members that Weston was working under a car when the train moved unexpectedly, without proper warning signals. His wife was at their boardinghouse nearby and reached him just in time to say goodbye before he died. (Courtesy Weston Estate.)

Sand Creek Ice Plant employees George Wright (left) and Ora Carmine pose for a photograph. Newton Ice Company supplied the Santa Fe Railroad in 1898, but railroad workers iced the cars. Local railroad historian Mike Hurley wrote that, in the first such contract a railroad ever signed, Newton Ice Company agreed that its employees would take over icing. The result was a new ice plant near Sand Creek Railroad Bridge. Iced refrigerator cars were called "reefers." Employees used chutes, chain hoists, tongs, and long wooden staffs to place 300-pound ice cakes and rock salt into compartments called bunkers in each end of the reefer. Heaters regulated temperatures inside the car and kept commodities from freezing. The Sand Creek Ice Plant was demolished in 1967. (Courtesy Ron Saunders.)

This Sand Creek yard office stood beside the main Santa Fe line to Dodge City. It was replaced in the 1930s with a more modern building, constructed to the left of this one. Local railroad historian L.E. Stagner estimated that 18 trains passed through the yard every 24 hours by the late 1930s. Additional trains came through during spring and fall livestock seasons and summer wheat harvest. (Courtesy Metcalf Sisters Antiques.)

The Santa Fe roundhouse, at top left, is a prominent feature in this aerial photograph of Newton taken in 1941 by the US Army Air Corps, 9th Photo Section, based at Fort Riley. The roundhouse closed in January 1955 and was torn down later that year. Stone from the destroyed roundhouse filled in old maintenance trenches and holes around tracks. (Courtesy Loyette Polhans Olson and Beverley Buller.)

In the foreground of this 1938 view of the Santa Fe and Fred Harvey facilities are, from left to right, Santa Fe fire hose cart building, Mexican section house No. 116, and the medical building for Mexican families. In the center are, from left to right, the Fred Harvey Dairy building, the Fred Harvey warehouse (with refrigeration plant on west end and cooling tower in back), and the Fred Harvey Produce building, which contained a carbonation plant and poultry operation. Before the Sand Creek yards were built in 1906, Mexican track workers lived in shanties called "tie houses" made from old railroad ties. Beginning in 1926, the railroad provided rent-free housing, called "section houses," because the inhabitants were workers on a section, or maintenance, gang. Workers and their families called the houses *ranchitos*. The two original brick houses had an adjacent building with toilets and running water, but there was no running water in the houses. Heat was by gas or coal stove, and light came from kerosene lamps. An "improved" third house containing a six-unit toilet was built in 1930. Inhabitants could shop at the railroad commissary, and a nurse, sometimes accompanied by a doctor, made scheduled visits to the medical building. Our Lady of Guadalupe Chapel was nearby. Most Mexicans moved out by the late 1950s, and the section houses were razed in the 1960s. The medical building was moved and became part of a ballfield concession stand. (Courtesy Harvey County Historical Museum and Archive.)

Glenn Patrick grew up in Newton. Upon his return to town from US Navy service in World War II, he found a shortage of jobs. But an exceptional wheat harvest opened up Santa Fe Railroad jobs in 1947. Patrick was only 20 years old when he signed on as a fireman. He left Santa Fe once and worked as an Amtrak engineer for 10 years, but returned to freight trains rather than accept a mandatory move to Kansas City. Eventually, he worked 52 years for Santa Fe and retired shortly after the railroad merged with Burlington Northern. Steam engines like this Prairie-type 2-6-2 coal-burning locomotive were still used when Patrick started. (Courtesy Glenn Patrick.)

Glenn Patrick, in window, and Fred Crawford, leaning from the gangway, pause for a photograph before beginning a 65-boxcar drag to Dodge City in August 1948. Patrick, 22, was a fireman for Santa Fe. He and two other men nearly froze to death later that year when an unexpected blizzard compromised communications and stranded trains at Satanta, Kansas. Patrick remembers a cloudy but windless morning when leaving Dodge City. Crewmembers left their winter clothes in the waycar, another name for the caboose, hitched 56 cars behind the engine. By 9:00 p.m., at Satanta, with heavy snow falling and 75-mile-per-hour winds blowing, Patrick and two others decided to leave the depot and try to make it to their waycar, where a brakeman and a conductor were waiting. They thought they could walk through the snow if they held on to each other, but became separated when they fell. Patrick, unable to hear the others over the storm's noise, turned back toward the depot, bumped into a train car, and found the two men huddled against a boxcar. They decided the waycar was closer, but repeatedly fell in snowdrifts and became too frozen and too weak to get up. Patrick saw the waycar's lights and crawled to it, but could not climb the steps. He managed to bang on the steps and made enough noise to alert the crew members inside, who came out and rescued all three men. The next morning, all of the trains were completely covered with snow. (Courtesy Glenn Patrick.)

The first diesel engine in Newton arrived on Christmas Day 1952. Retired engineer Glenn Patrick said "the difference was like night and day" between steam and diesel. Although steam and early diesel were nearly equal in power, most steam engines could not pull more than 80 cars, and Patrick said additional engines and crews had to be added for longer trains. Diesel technology reduced the need for additional manpower because several engines could be operated by a single crew in the lead engine. (Courtesy Glenn Patrick.)

The Texas Chief (at right), once one of the premier passenger trains of the Santa Fe Railroad, makes a stop at Newton Station. This particular engine was used through the 1950s, when about 15 passenger trains passed through Newton each day. (Courtesy Harvey County Historical Museum and Archive.)

When trains added dining cars, Harvey House restaurants fed local residents instead of rail travelers. Helen Collins, shown here, was 18 years old in August 1953 when she became a waitress, also called a "Harvey Girl." The original Harvey Girls responded to Fred Harvey's advertisements in Eastern newspapers calling for "young women of good character." The girls were required to live in company housing, remain unmarried for a specified time, and follow a strict code of conduct. Like most modern Harvey Girls, Helen was married when hired. She stayed until the restaurant closed, despite protests from local officials and residents, on May 5, 1957. The restaurant was leased out twice, though not as part of the Harvey chain, then closed permanently in 1979. (Courtesy Helen Collins.)

Harvey Girls celebrate Christmas 1953 at Newton. From left to right are Kay Brown, Frances Okle, hostess Elizabeth McMadney, and Clare Conner. Fred Harvey's great-grandson Daggett Harvey visited Hutchinson (Kansas) Community College in 1982 for a Harvey Girls reunion, attended by about 70 former Harvey Girls. (Courtesy Helen Collins.)

Frank Little Jr., a passenger conductor for the Santa Fe Railroad, spent the last years of his career working between Newton and Dodge City. This photograph of him at Newton Station appeared on the July 1955 cover of *Santa Fe* magazine. The train stopped next to him is train No. 19, called the Chief. (Courtesy Dan Hollingshead and Patti Little Hollingshead.)

Dan Hollingshead, three or four years old, sits with his grandfather Homer Watkins in the cab of a burro crane in Newton's rail mill yard, while other rail mill workers pose outside. Watkins was a veteran crane operator, and Hollingshead remembers being taken to the yard, often with his sister, for photographs like this one from 1955 or 1956. The rail mill salvaged reclaimed rails and other materials. According to local railroad historian Mike Hurley, materials from Newton's mill were once used throughout the Santa Fe system. (Courtesy Dan Hollingshead.)

James Patrick (left), 16 at the time, received special permission from Burlington Northern Santa Fe Railroad to accompany his father, Glenn Patrick, on his final run as an engineer on March 15, 1999. The company surprised Glenn with a brand-new, fresh-from-the-factory engine for the occasion. (Courtesy Glenn Patrick.)

Glenn Patrick waves to a friend in Hutchinson, Kansas, on his last run as a Burlington Northern Santa Fe engineer after 52 injury-free years of service on the railroad. (Courtesy Glenn Patrick.)

Three

BUSINESS AS USUAL IN NEWTON

Newton grew beside the railroad tracks. A Main Street business section, despite frequent interruption in traffic from freight trains, remains active today.

From the time Peter Luhn located his pioneer store in Newton in the 1870s, to now, a succession of businesses has come and gone. Some types, like blacksmiths and carriage factories, faded as technology changed. Others, like car dealerships, moved out of the central business district when interstate highways created new traffic patterns. There are no downtown hotels now, as train passengers do not stop overnight in Newton anymore.

There are few locally owned clothing shops, no shoe stores, no department stores, no movie theatres, and no drug stores downtown. Their replacements include antique shops, art galleries, and offices. Vestiges of earlier times remain, including local banks. There are still a few bookstores, especially Anderson's, which has been in business more than a century. A dollar store replaced the downtown grocery stores, but if a shopper goes just past the flour mill, on the very edge of old downtown, a former neighborhood grocery has become a small meat market. Bread can also be obtained there, at a local restaurant, and at a health food store that carries some produce. A few eateries remain. Neighborhood groceries have been replaced by chain stores placed at strategic intersections.

All this could change. Newton Medical Center, one of the largest employers in town, is south of the old section of Newton. An outlet mall built not far beyond it in the 1990s now houses Newton's only movie theater. In between, one finds Wal-Mart, a farm store, and a strip mall, and more new residential development is moving in that direction.

Such neighborhood growth is the story of today and tomorrow. Yesterday, it was business as usual in Newton.

A disagreement over the price of quinine in 1871 resulted in the establishment of Dickey's Drug Store. J.B. Dickey, a doctor's son who worked in drugstores in other states before he decided to try handling cattle, suffered chills and fever while working in the Arkansas River bottomland. His solution to his dispute with W.P. Pugh, who had just opened the store, was to purchase the entire place. When the store burned down the following year, Dickey telegraphed for new stock while the building was still in flames and found a new location. He later built his own building and added a jewelry business. Two of his sons became pharmacists and continued the store. (Courtesy Mennonite Library and Archives.)

One of Dickey's competitors was Reese Drug Store, which also opened in the early days of Newton. It stocked drugs and jewelry, and was left by owner John Reese Sr. to his two sons. The Italianate style Reese home on East First Street is now a historic landmark. (Courtesy Harvey County Historical Museum and Archive.)

Howard Starr Dickey, one of J.B. Dickey's sons, did not become a pharmacist. Instead, he opened a book and music shop. In addition to placing pianos in many Newton homes, Howard Dickey wrote songs and magazine and newspaper stories. The back cover of this Mother's Day song he published in 1920 advertises his other compositions. (Courtesy Dena Bisnette.)

Now known as Old Mill Plaza on Main Street, this Newton landmark, seen here at rear center, was built in 1879 as Monarch Steam Mill. Bernard Warkentin bought it in 1886, renamed it Newton Milling and Elevator Company, and changed it to a roller mill. Pictured here about 1900, the mill eventually closed and most of the mansard roof had actually been demolished by the time local residents Lloyd and Jacqueline Smith rescued the building in the 1970s and renovated it for adaptive reuse. Today, the Old Mill houses a restaurant and offices. (Courtesy Warkentin House Museum.)

"STARR" Songs Please Everybody

You can get other beautiful Ballads

Written and Composed by

Howard ★ Dickey

"Publisher of 'STARR' songs"
Newton, Kansas

"The Old Home On The Hill"
Waltz time and A wonderful Appealing Song.

Starr Dickey's "BACK HOME" Song
This Song is a positive Hit. Waltz time.

"When You Come Out Into The Sunshine Again, I'll Still Be Waiting For You."
This song appeals to all classes of people and is well worth buying

"What I Like To Be Called."
A very pretty song in waltz time, that young folks love to sing.

"The Only Song I Can Remember"
The finest Mother Song ever written. If you loved your mother you'll want this song.

"Till the Rainbow Colors Shine Clear Across The Sky"
A Ballad of Faith and Hope in Beautifully expressed words and music.

"When The Nightingale Sings in the Moonlight."
This song is as pretty a sentimental song as you'll hear in a lifetime.

Fulfillment
A Grand song as the title indicates.

"That Gee Gee Girl of Mine."
A Fox Trot that is simply delightful

Any of the above songs will be sent postpaid for 30c a copy or 3 copies for $1.00.
If you cannot obtain these songs from your local dealer, send postage stamps for as many as you want, to

Howard Starr Dickey
Publisher of "STARR" songs
Newton, Kansas

Two workers have their photograph taken with an unfinished carriage at J.J. Krehbiel's Carriage Factory. John Jacob Krehbiel moved to Newton in 1879. He and George Epps operated Angood Blacksmith Shop at 128 East Sixth. In 1883, Krehbiel bought out Epps and erected a two-story building for his new carriage factory. He ran the company until giving it to his eldest son, Edgar, who operated it for another 18 years. Today, the Carriage Factory is an example of adaptive reuse, housing an art gallery. (Courtesy Mennonite Library and Archives.)

Another son of J.J. Krehbiel, Albert Henry Krehbiel, trained as a carriage maker, but became an artist, painting murals and landscapes. The Carriage Factory Art Gallery displays some of his works. His distinctive styles include rain, fog, and snow in air. Krehbiel attended the School of Design and Painting in Topeka and the Art Institute of Chicago, and studied in Paris with Jean Paul Laurens at Julian Academy. He won the prestigious Prix de Rome and other awards and had two paintings displayed in the Louvre in Paris. He was an Art Institute of Chicago instructor from 1905 until his death in 1945. (Courtesy Carriage Factory Art Gallery.)

Dr. John Thomas Axtell, who first practiced upstairs in Dickey's Drug Store, established Axtell Hospital in 1887 on his own land in the 200 block of Broadway. Later, he added Axtell Clinic. His wife, Dr. Lucena Chase Axtell, and Dr. Frank L. Abbey practiced with him. Lucena managed to attended medical school in Kansas City while raising four children and assisting her husband. Knowing that women needed opportunities to become health-care professionals, the Axtells opened the Axtell School of Nursing, with Lucena as director. The school was the first for registered nurses in Kansas. Axtell gave his hospital to the state convention of Disciples of Christ in 1924, which then changed its name to Axtell Christian Hospital. A 1987 merger with Bethel Deaconess Hospital created Newton Medical Center. (Courtesy John Wiebe.)

Mennonite Mutual Fire Insurance incorporated in 1880. The first directors were David Goerz, Herman Suderman, Peter Harms, John Siemens, and Jacob W. Regier. The neoclassical building shown here was constructed in 1915. These last names are familiar to Newton residents because descendants of these pioneer families still live in town. (Courtesy Mennonite Library and Archive.)

Now called Anderson Office Supply, the store local residents simply call "Anderson's" is the oldest continuously operating family-owned business in Newton. Phillip Murray Anderson sold newspapers on Santa Fe trains in 1892. Two years later, he turned a piano box into a news and refreshment stand at 420 Main, selling sandwiches made by his mother, Clarissa. In 1900, he moved to a double storefront where the railroad depot is now. His store became the first in town to sell Victrolas, General Electric refrigerators, Hallmark cards, Kodak photofinishing services, fireworks, and school textbooks. He also sold china in a second shop, shown here on the left next to the 1900–1928 store at 422-424 Main Street. Anderson's moved to 522 Main Street in 1928 and to its present location in the old Becker Brothers Grocery at 627 North Main in 1938. A loft constructed in a different location was moved to the new store. Anderson's grandson Phil Anderson features local history books and sports items in addition to office supplies. (Courtesy Phil Anderson.)

Lee & McDaniel Furniture, purveyors of both new and secondhand furniture, was downtown near the Old Mill. The three-story building at 227 North Main, eventually demolished, looked like this in 1900. The shop windows advertise a Ringling Brothers Circus. Later, the store became Harrison Furniture and had a hotel upstairs. (Courtesy Thelma Weston Estate.)

The Railroad Building, Loan, and Savings Association was organized in June 1896 by a group of railroad men who wanted to help employees set up homes in Newton. After renting a series of offices, including one in the Masonic lodge, the company moved in 1915 to a Beaux-Arts building at the corner of Fifth and Main Streets. It was designed by Newton native Samuel Greenebaum. Now known as the "500 Main Place," it serves as headquarters for the Newton Area Chamber of Commerce and several businesses. (Courtesy Loyette Polhans Olson and Beverley Buller.)

Best Equipped Shop in
Newton Kans.
C. R. Gray, Prop.

Charles Russell Gray operated a blacksmith and woodwork shop at 208 West Second Street. He opened it in 1905, after having learned his trade by working with other blacksmiths. He had also handled blacksmithing and horseshoeing for A. Moore's railroad grading camp. In many cases, the local blacksmith became the local automobile mechanic after cars became more numerous than horses. Although Gray modernized his equipment with power machines and electric motors, he kept his business strictly blacksmithing and horseshoeing. (Courtesy Karen Jacobson.)

S.A. Hanlin arrived in Newton in 1890 and started a store that grew into Hanlin Supply & Mercantile Company. At one time, he supplied provisions for the Santa Fe's commissary cars. He also operated a grocery and mercantile with J.J. Lewis. Hanlin's store eventually took up a whole building at 601 North Main and was advertised as "the largest cash department store in the state." In the 1920s, the store became Cayot Mercantile. (Courtesy Harvey County Historical Museum and Archive.)

Rich Mercantile Company operated in downtown Newton from the early 1900s until the 1940s and featured merchandise including cars, tractors, and Kelvinator and Maytag appliances. William Joseph Rich, the owner, stands just left of the tractor in this photograph from about 1920. His son Willis Rich, holding a stick over his right shoulder, stands near the tractor. William's daughter Selma and his wife, Lina, are on the sidewalk behind Willis. During World War II, because the family's heritage was German and Mennonite, the store was vandalized. In addition to smashed windows and damaged merchandise, yellow paint was spread around because Mennonites are traditionally pacifists. A relative to the family by marriage, flight officer Ed O'Dell decided to send a message to the vandals by showing up in uniform to help with the cleanup. (Courtesy Zona Galle.)

New farm machines arrive at W.J. Rich & Company on West Broadway, drawing a crowd of curious spectators. Just above the Rich sign is one indicating that he is a dealer for Studebaker buggies, once considered the best in the country. (McDaniel Studios photograph; courtesy Mennonite Archives and Library.)

John Russell and his partner, Edd Stellers, ran this meat market on South Main Street in Newton. (Courtesy Thelma Weston Estate.)

Carl Russell drives a delivery wagon through Newton, displaying product advertising on a blanket draped over his mule. He is stopped in front of McManus Brothers, a well-known department store that was a fixture in downtown Newton for many years. (Courtesy Weston Estate.)

Kansas State Bank opened in 1902. Its first president was Bernard Warkentin, and C.F. Claassen served as its first vice president. The three-story building stood at the corner of Sixth and Main Streets. It was one of several locally owned banks in turn-of-the-century Newton. (Courtesy Karen Jacobson.)

The Newton Fire Department was originally located on the present-day site of Newton Recreation Center. In the days before trucks, members of the fire department included horses. George Bausman is on the back of the wagon, while Chief O.N. Eberly leans against it and E.C. Warhurst drives in this photograph from 1907. Today's fire department has expanded to three stations. (Courtesy John Wiebe.)

Clara Wagner, daughter of Star Theatre owner Ed Wagner, runs the projector in about 1915. The "rays" coming from the projector were scratched onto the photograph's negative. The Star Theatre, later renamed Fox Theatre, is the subject of a continuing restoration project. (Courtesy Harvey County Historical Museum and Archive.)

Bethel Deaconess Hospital was dedicated on June 11, 1908. Sr. Frieda Kaufman became the first superintendent. Later that year, Bethel Deaconess Hospital School of Nursing opened and became an integral part of hospital operations. The original 30-bed facility received three additions between its founding and 1950, and a separate school building was constructed. Bethel merged with Axtell Christian Hospital on January 1, 1988, becoming Newton Medical Center. (Courtesy Loyette Polhans Olson and Beverley Buller.)

Another Newton landmark, Midland National Bank, opened in 1893 on the corner of Fifth and Main Streets. Three years later, bank officials spent $6,000 on a new site, at 527 North Main, and the bank moved there in 1907. Herman E. Suderman, who came to the United States from Russia in 1885, started at German National Bank as a messenger boy and janitor when he was 13 years old. In 1902, he went to work for Midland Bank, becoming a director and vice president in 1903. He bought a controlling interest in 1916 and became bank president in 1919. His son John succeeded him in 1954, and members of the Suderman family continue their association with the bank. (Courtesy John Wiebe.)

A 1910 statement from Midland National Bank details its resources and liabilities, which came out even for the first quarter of the year. The recipient of this postcard, E.P. Barrows of nearby Sedgwick, either was a stockholder or had an account at Midland. (Courtesy Karen Jacobson.)

Hogan's store, known as "The Racket," specialized in "A Little Bit of Everything" from 1913 until 1970. R.L. Hogan, a former traveling salesman, bought out his partner, J.S. Brenner, five years after purchasing an existing store from S.A. Davis. Hogan bought a store in Peabody and partnered in a store at Herrington to increase the amount of merchandise he could buy at one time, passing the savings on to customers. In 10 years, the store grew so much that it required six full-time clerks. Hogan always kept a German-speaking clerk, and he was the first businessman in town to hire African American and Mexican American employees. In 1945, he gave the business to his eldest son, Morris. (Courtesy Harvey County Historical Museum and Archive.)

The proprietors of Toevs Bros. Grocery, at 212 Main Street, and an unidentified woman, greet customers about 1910. The two men are G.R. Toevs (center) and Paul Entz (right), who subsequently opened his own grocery store. The storefront features advertisements for soap and a circus. (Courtesy Mennonite Library and Archives.)

J.M. "Joe" Supernois designed window displays for many of Newton's Main Street shops during the 1920s. He kept pictures of many of his favorites. This display, at the F.W. Woolworth Company Store, advertised its fall sale in October 1923. (Courtesy Monica Supernois.)

Velma Kratzen (left) is pictured with Joe Supernois inside Cayot Mercantile Company at the old Hanlin's building on the northwest corner of Sixth and Main Streets in 1928. Later, a J.C. Penney store moved in. Afterward, the building was modified for adaptive reuse and now houses several businesses, including Prairie Harvest, a locally run health food store that also serves lunch and dinner. (Courtesy Monica Supernois.)

Joe Supernois designed window displays for Cayot Merchantile, including this one in the spring of 1928. He and other employees competed each season for the best window, and the prize was a cash bonus. This one advertises a brand still familiar to many shoppers today, Arrow Shirts. The price posted here for a dress shirt is $1.95. (Courtesy Monica Supernois.)

William Ramey stands ready to serve customers at the Texaco station at 327 West Broadway around 1936. Gerald S. Kelso owned the station from its opening in 1935 until his death in 1967. Kelso also served as area jobber (distributor) for Texaco products. Karen Jacobson, Kelso's daughter, said her parents raised horses before starting the gasoline business, but sold the horses and moved to town so she could attend school. (Courtesy Karen Jacobson.)

While he was laid off from his job at the Santa Fe roundhouse shops, Walter Groves operated the Conoco station at the southeast corner of Second Street. This photograph was taken during the early 1930s. Gasoline stations, like neighborhood grocery stores, were once scattered all over Newton. (Courtesy Karen Jacobson.)

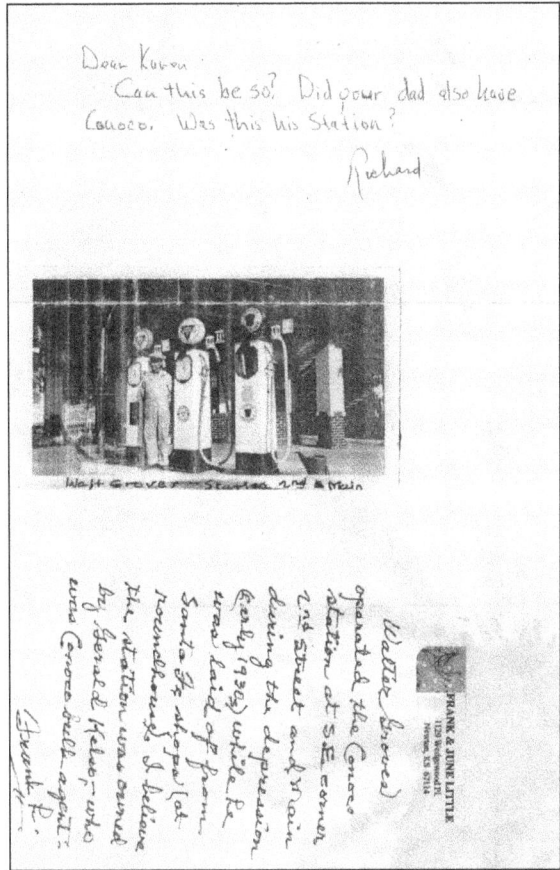

Dear Karen:
Can this be so? Did your dad also have Conoco. Was this his Station?
Richard

Walter Groves
operated the Conoco station at S.E. corner 2nd Street and Main during the depression (early 1930s) while he was laid off from Santa Fe shops (at roundhouse). I believe the station was owned by Gerald Kelver who was Conoco bull agent.
Frank R.

PRANK & JUNE LITTLE
1129 Wedgewood Pl.
Newton, KS 67114

Thelma Weston (right) ran the Selective Service Office, commonly known as the draft board. Here, Thelma and an unidentified woman, probably a coworker, pause for a photograph in front of the office. (Courtesy Thelma Weston Estate.)

Charles Kenneth Weston shows off the truck he drove for McGee's Potato Chips in 1947. McGee's chips were made in Newton. The business originally started on West Fifth Street, but later moved to a second location in town. (Courtesy Weston Estate.)

Flour mills are a traditional employer in wheat-producing states, and although Goerz Mill has changed its name and appearance several times, it continues to operate, now as Horizon Milling. Built in 1918 by Rudolf Goerz, it is one of only 10 working flour mills left in Kansas. Other Newton mills included Eagle (later Superior) Mill, which burned in the 1960s; and Claassen Flour Mill, demolished in 1963 to make room for a Kansas Gas and Electric office. (Courtesy Mennonite Library and Archives.)

Joe and Molly Supernois opened a furniture store at 224 North Main Street in 1936, taking in three storefronts, including a Safeway Grocery. The family still owns their building on the corner of Main and Second Streets, including apartments upstairs. In this 1952 photograph, the tin ceiling and loft are seen behind Joe and Molly's daughter-in-law Normadeen, who ran the store with her husband, Calvin Supernois. Metcalf Sisters Antiques now occupies the ground floor, where original interior architecture, including the ceiling and loft, remains. In 1895, the same building housed Powell and Krueger Grocery. When Z.E. Powell died in 1910, the business passed to W.A. Krueger Sr., who added shoes and dry goods. W.A. Krueger Jr. owned the store into the 1920s. (Courtesy Monica Supernois.)

Johnny Mears ran the downtown confectionery known as Princess Sweet Shop, at 518 Main Street. He is shown here around 1943. Such shops were popular in the 1930s, 1940s, and 1950s. Another favorite in Newton was Candyland, which in the 1930s posted its sign, barber-pole style, on a giant wooden peppermint stick. (Harvey County Historical Museum and Archive.)

Calvin Lee Supernois (left) and Joe Supernois pose on a sunny afternoon in 1946 in front of their third storefront, a resale room for new and used furniture. Beginning at the corner of Third and Main Streets were Supernois Furniture, the second store the family called "the lamp store," and this one, which had the motto, "If you want it, we have it. If you have it, we want it." The sign above, "Norge," was left over from a previous business. (Courtesy Monica Supernois.)

Joe Supernois erected a second building, at 123 East Broadway, shown here under construction in June 1949. Originally operated by his son, Calvin, as a furniture store, it was later sold to a family named Collier. It also once housed a Western Auto store. The name "Supernois" can still be seen in the light-colored block on the left corner of the building. Today, the structure is home to Bethel College Academy of Performing Arts and Hershberger Piano Gallery. (Courtesy Monica Supernois.)

Avery-Hurst Motors shows the newest General Motors product in its display window on East Fourth Street. All of the downtown automobile dealerships have moved away from the main downtown section of Newton. Defunct car dealerships remembered in the area also include the original Hurst Ford dealership and Holstine's. (Harvey County Historical Museum and Archives.)

Mr. and Mrs. Henry Walters stand proudly in front of their downtown shoe store in 1950. (Courtesy Monica Supernois.)

In 1950, Rupert Hohman (left) and Ralph Sundquist operate machines at Mennonite Press, one of Newton's oldest businesses. It opened in 1902 as Bethel College Print Shop. In 1949, the college joined with the board of publication of the General Conference Mennonite Church and incorporated the business as the nonprofit Mennonite Press. In 1971, it became a for-profit and was eventually sold. Roger Williams, one of the buyers, served as managing director from 1978 to 1983. Another, Steve Rudiger, succeeded him. (Courtesy Mennonite Press Inc.)

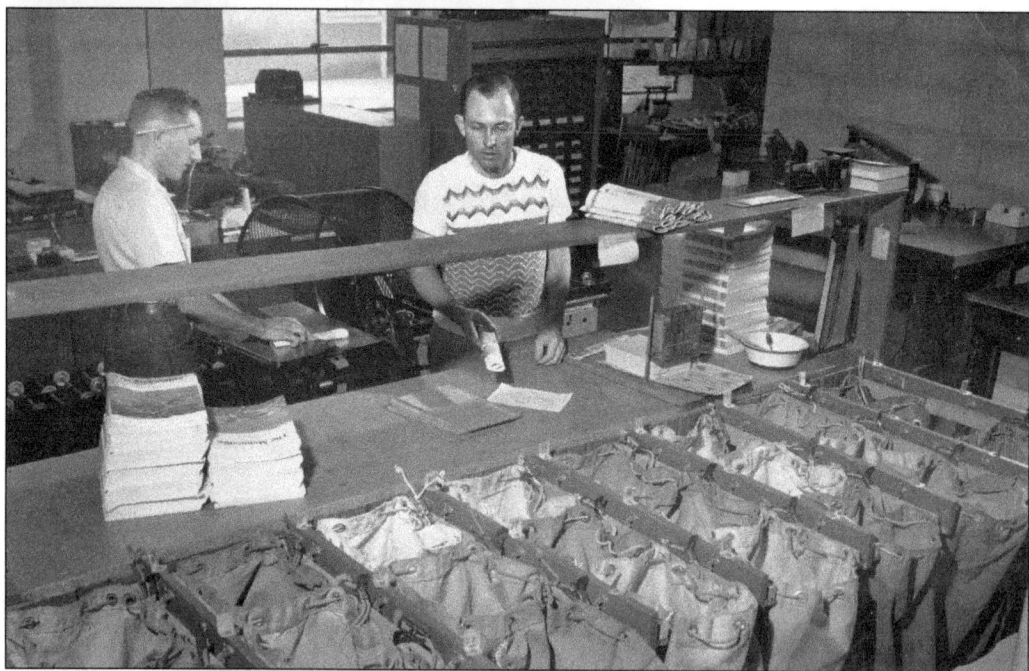

Galen Rudiger (left) and Harold Bartel work in the mailroom in the Grattan Building, the second headquarters of Mennonite Press. The first was the Science Hall at Bethel College. The Grattan Building, across from Bethel College, also housed a grocery store. (Courtesy Mennonite Press Inc.)

Steve Rudiger checks a page layout at Mennonite Press in 1974. Continued expansion led to relocation again, and Mennonite Press now operates at 532 North Oliver Road near the Newton Airport. During World War II, the airport was taken over by the Navy as part of Hutchinson Naval Air Station. Newton officials later asked for it back, and it is a civilian airport again. (Courtesy Mennonite Press Inc.)

Longtime Newton residents remember downtown as crowded, especially on Saturdays. On the corner at left is the city auditorium, often the reason for a long line of people in the first block of West Sixth Street. On this particular day, however, a sale at Montgomery Ward appears to be the center of attraction. The stone building between the auditorium and Montgomery Ward was Worton Memorials. (Courtesy John Wiebe.)

Fallen snow surrounds the office of the Ancient Order of United Workmen, at 401 East First Street. The name changed later to First Kansas Life Insurance Association. Many insurance agencies started as fraternal organizations operating benevolent funds for their members. (Courtesy Harvey County Historical Museum and Archive.)

Two typesetters work at Herald Publishing Company in October 1950. Herald Publishing started as Herold Bookstore and published *Der Herold*, a German-language newspaper for local Mennonites. In 1923, the company began a second publication, *Mennonite Weekly Review*, in English. *Der Herold* was discontinued in December 1941 due to anti-German sentiment with the onset of World War II. (Courtesy Bethany Mace and Rosie Wiebe.)

Robert Wiebe works at his desk at Herald Publishing Company in about 1950. The company changed its name to match that of its major publication, *Mennonite Weekly Review*. The firm, at West Sixth Street, continues to produce publications for a predominantly Mennonite audience. (Courtesy Bethany Mace and Rosie Wiebe.)

Quality Bakery was one of many bakeries in Newton over the years. One bakery that was in operation when Newton turned 50 in 1922 was called Perfect Bakery. Older residents remember another establishment, Pandandy Bakery. One of the first three businesses in Newton was a bakery. (Courtesy Catherine French.)

Moore's IGA store was one of more than 25 grocery stores that have come and gone in Newton. The last one, Boese Grocery on South Kansas Street, closed in 1991. Gillispie's Grocery still exists as a meat market. (Courtesy Harvey County Historical Museum and Archive.)

The Harvey County Courthouse looms over the construction site for its replacement in this July 1964 *Newton Kansan* newspaper photograph. The courthouse tower had been a prominent feature of Newton's skyline since 1907. The site was donated in 1878, but county offices moved several times before construction was completed. In 1905, the Kansas legislature approved a special county tax to finance construction, and in 1906, the county bought three lots next to the donated property at Eighth and Main Streets. The cornerstone-laying ceremony was accompanied by a parade, speeches, and placement of artifacts into the cornerstone. (Courtesy Karen Wall.)

Guest House Self-Service Cafeteria, in the 600 block of Main Street, became Newton's first integrated restaurant in 1957, when one of the owners, James Rutschman, saw African American railroad porters looking for a place to eat and invited them inside. Later, Rutschman traveled to Chicago and his kindness was repaid. A porter recognized Rutschman, who was lost. He helped Rutschman get around the city until he got on the train back to Newton. Bethel College professor Dr. J. Winfield Fretz originally opened the Guest House, Newton's first buffet, and took on Rutschman as a business partner. (Courtesy Mennonite Library and Archive.)

Karen Wall, daughter of Sheriff Russell Werner, grew up in the front part of the old Harvey County Jail building, shown here in the early 1960s. The front was the sheriff's residence, and the back housed about 20 prisoners for up to a year each. After a year, they were transferred to the state prison. The Newton Police Department housed short-term prisoners. Wall remembers the place as "a wonderful, big, old house." It was torn down in 1965, the same year the old Harvey County Courthouse was demolished. (Courtesy Karen Wall.)

Normadeen and Calvin Supernois, shown here in 1977, allowed customers to use the rear door of their furniture store at the alley off of Second Street. Many of Newton's downtown commercial buildings, like this one, have apartments upstairs, some of which are still inhabited. Although the upper stories of some of the other downtown buildings have fallen into disrepair or have been converted into storage space, a recent redevelopment push in the Downtown Historic District has resulted in rehabilitation of several second floors. At several locations, metal false facades put up during the 1950s have been removed to reveal original brick walls and windows covered for decades. Today, the Supernois building retains its 1950s appearance, including its corrugated metal false facade. (Courtesy Monica Supernois.)

Four

NEWTON AT WAR

Wartime in Newton was much like wartime in any other railroad town. Local residents realized that soldiers would be moving through on trains, and pitched in to make what might be a serviceman's last memory of home as pleasant as possible.

Red Cross canteens and USO groups were started. Churches, businesses, and social organizations got involved. People crowded the station to greet the soldiers when trains stopped in town. One local man who worked at the Harvey House restaurant remembers making box lunches to sell to soldiers on the train.

Most men and some women went off to war. Those who stayed home often worked in a war-related job. Newton's proximity to Wichita meant that many of those jobs were in the aircraft industry. A few ladies who played the role of "Rosie the Riveter" still live in Newton and remember a bus sent from Wichita to take them to work building airplanes.

Sometimes, war can be good for business. It certainly kept the Santa Fe Railroad busy. Additional freights came through carrying war materiel, but the biggest impact was on passenger service. In peacetime, more than a dozen passenger trains came through Newton every day, but during wars that number was increased by troop trains. A local railroad historian recorded more than 40 trains a day during the nationwide peak of rail travel in World War II.

Some of those who went to war returned. Some did not, and Newton has public memorials to the fallen. People still go to war, but they do not depart on trains anymore. Now, most of the military men and women who leave home with memories of Newton are the ones who grew up in town.

Newton residents buy World War I bonds at a curbside booth at Sixth and Main Streets near Kansas State Bank, visible in the background at right. The booth is decorated with posters and four flags and a bell on the roof. One poster says "Save—Buy—For Victory" while another depicts an eagle and says "Keep Him Free." The men include J.D. Nicholson, who was treasurer of the Red Cross; J.C. Nicholson; and one-time postmaster Josiah Foltz, second from left. (Courtesy Harvey County Historical Society and Archive.)

Newton's Red Cross Canteen became an important gathering place for local residents who wanted to support the troops during the world wars. It was conveniently located downtown, just a short walk from the railroad depot. (Courtesy Loyette Polhans Olson and Beverley Buller.)

As a railroad town, Newton saw many troop trains passing through during both World War I and World War II. Local ladies provided refreshments and encouragement to the military personnel. This group worked out of the Red Cross Canteen and included Lina Rich, standing sixth from left. (Courtesy Zona Galle.)

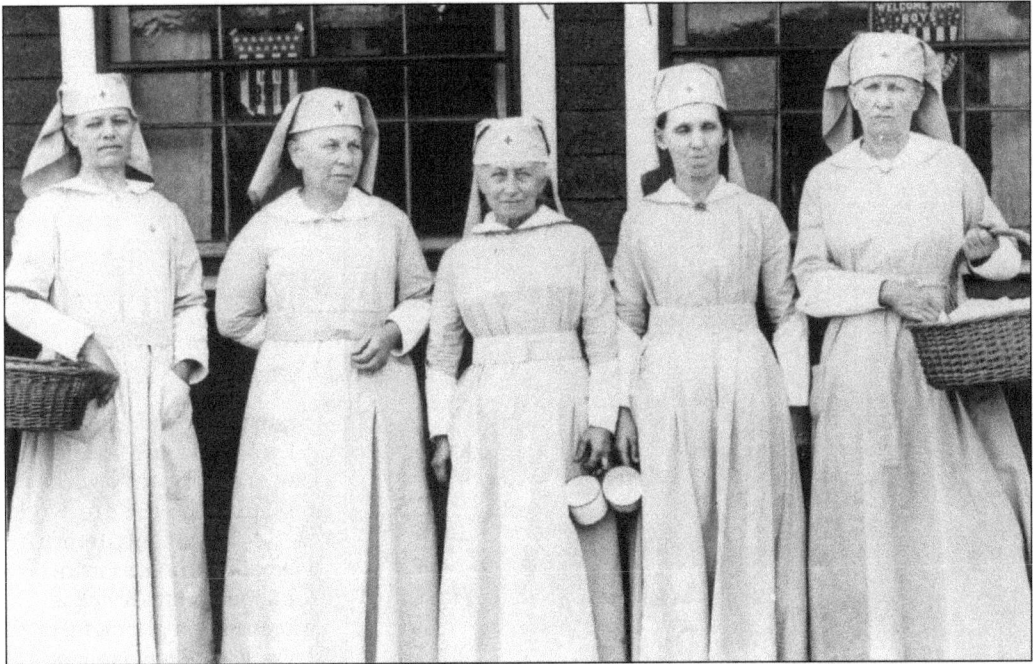

Volunteers from Zion Lutheran Church prepare to meet returning World War I soldiers at Newton's Red Cross Canteen. Shown here are, from left to right, Mrs. H.A. Meets, Emma Brauer, Mary Hoyer, Mrs. Don Hauck, and Mrs. Fred Hartenberger. Ladies from local churches and social organizations helped at the canteen. (Courtesy Zion Lutheran Church.)

This bench in front of the courthouse, commemorating those who died in World War I, is one of the many military monuments around Newton. Members of the Order of the Gold Star, who provided this memorial, were mothers who had lost their sons in the war. (Jim Wimmer photograph.)

Seaman Second Class Victor Otis Hays was just one of the many Newton residents who went to World War II and did not return. Here, an announcement for a memorial service is attached to a photograph Hays sent home. He was killed in action aboard the USS *Neches* on January 23, 1942. (Courtesy First Baptist Church.)

War took many Newton residents far from home. Glenn Patrick, who grew up in Newton, still keeps a photograph of the ship on which he served. Patrick was a helmsman who manned a 22-millimeter gun on the USS Patrol Craft 790, a submarine hunter. After the war, Patrick had a career as a railroad engineer. (Courtesy Glenn Patrick.)

Newton resident Harry Kasitz enlisted in the US Army Air Corps and trained at Fort Riley, but received a medical discharge when a leg he had broken twice during childhood kept him from completing an obstacle course. Kasitz was hired in 1940 by Dwayne Wallace at Cessna and worked in the aircraft industry for 24 years. He remembers that Cessna had about 200 workers in July 1940 and that the number grew to about 2,000 by April 1941. His first job at the company was in the woodwork building, constructing wing spars. (Courtesy Harry Kasitz.)

Fred E. Killfoil, shown here as a member of the Civilian Conservation Corps during the Great Depression, served in the US Army during World War II and settled in Newton upon his return. Killfoil, originally from Lakin, is 13th from the left in the fourth row in this photograph of the Traveling Jayhawks, 1764th Company, CCC Bonanza Camp F-83. The CCC was a government agency that employed young men to work on roads, bridges, and national park facilities in the 1930s. After leaving the CCC, Killfoil married, and he and his wife were on their way home to Lakin one day in the 1930s when their car broke down in Harvey County. After doing some farm work, Killfoil was hired by a flour mill in Halstead. After the war, he worked at the Santa Fe rail mill in Newton until his retirement in 1977. (Courtesy Mary Hanke.)

Another serviceman who made it back from war was Gene Miles, shown here surrounded by young ladies. From left to right are (first row) Adelaide Deschner, Miles, and Miss Brown; (second row) unidentified, Betty Pond, Pearl Kerr, and Margaret, who later became Mrs. Miles. (Courtesy First Baptist Church.)

In October 1942, Newton Lutheran Canteen Team No. 7 included, from left to right: (first row) Frieda Stahl, Mary Ruff, Fena Freelich, Augusta Hauck, Helen Drogemuller, Dorothy Ratzlaff, Helen Lolmough, Catherine Walters, Coila Hartenberger, Rozena Broadhagen, unidentified, and Otilia Thimm; (second row) Hulda Steffen, Elizabeth Heine, Tillie Chapple, Louise Mashoff, Marie Zizman, Mary Bernhardt, Carolyn Buss, Florence Wilms, Mrs. J.H. Hawkins, and Elizabeth Myer; (third row) unidentified, Minnie Groneman, Nettie Ollenberger, Jeannie Fry, Esther Rodefeld, Sophia Struebing, Dora Lettau, Carrie Harms, Hulda Knittel, and Henriette Gradert. Additional volunteers not pictured include Estelle Raffety, Mrs. George Ohlander, Mrs. George Lowe, Mrs. Hollis Thomas, Alma Gradert, Grace Froelich, Mrs. Neal Stelljes, Alma Schmidt, Marie Kalthoff, Mrs. Ebert, Marie Froelich, Elnora Riffel, Roberta Macklem, Mrs. J. Smith, Mrs. Glenn Steele, and Betty Boldenow. (Courtesy Zion Lutheran Church.)

The 1942–1945 Baptist Canteen Group strikes a cheerful pose for the camera in front of the Newton Red Cross Canteen. Servicemen on the trains that stopped at Newton never had to worry about finding a friendly face at the station. Volunteers and the general public were always on hand to meet troop trains. (Courtesy First Baptist Church.)

AID TO U.S. NAVY
PLANE IDENTIFICATION
FredHarvey

During World War II, civilians were expected to help the war effort in every possible way. One way was staying alert for enemy activity at home. This card was on the tables in Harvey House restaurants to help the public learn how to recognize airplane silhouettes. This particular card came from Kansas City, but the same one would have been seen in Newton. (Courtesy Helen Collins.)

A crowd waits for a train to arrive at the Newton depot. While the trains often attracted attention because they brought celebrities, including politicians and actors, to town, they also brought troops going to or returning from war. In the 1940s, when this photograph was taken, people showed their support by being at the station to greet the trains. (Courtesy Dr. Gil Michel.)

Maurice W. Hind grew up in Newton and served in the US Army in the 1960s. Later, he followed in the footsteps of his father, M.B. Hind, and became a Newton Police Department officer. (Courtesy Val and Maurice Hind.)

The Reverend Louis Dale and Brig. Gen. Elizabeth Hoisington visit at First Presbyterian Church after raising the flag during Newton's centennial in 1971. General Hoisington joined the US Women's Army Corps in 1942 and was sent to Europe in 1944. She was promoted to brigadier general on June 11, 1970, the first woman to reach that rank. She died in 2007 and is buried at Arlington National Cemetery. Her father was Col. P.M. Hoisington, an early member of First Presbyterian Church. He had arranged for his daughter to be born in Newton, even though the family had moved. (Courtesy First Presbyterian Church.)

Five

NEWTON AT HOME AND AT SCHOOL

Early Newton experienced two major residential building booms. The first, in the 1880s, was spurred by the population growth of a developing town. Some homes belonging to founding families still exist, including many in the McKinley Residential Historic District, named for the local school, and more near the Downtown Historic District.

Nationwide financial panic in 1890 slowed economic growth, stalling home construction for almost two decades. Another construction surge began about 1910 and stretched into the 1920s, a period when several local schools were built. The Great Depression and conservation of materials during World War II were later influences on the building business, as was a population surge when soldiers returned and a third construction boom in the 1950s added several residential additions and new schools.

Newton became involved in the mobile home industry in the 1960s and 1970s, with several factories here. Some even lured workers away from the Santa Fe Railroad, but, eventually, that market faded and the factories closed.

Newton has as many styles of architecture as it has types of people. There is even a Lustron home, a rare structure made entirely of metal. Styles ranging from Queen Anne Victorians and craftsman bungalows to houses built from Sears and Roebuck plans purchased out of catalogs abound. Few neighborhoods are purely of one type or another.

Most African Americans arriving in Newton in 1871 were valued for their work skills and faced little discrimination, but by 1902 they lived only in a few specific neighborhoods. In the early 1900s, African Americans had their own business district centered in the 100 block of Fourth Street, but Mexicans initially were not even allowed to buy homes. The first recorded Mexican families arrived about 1910 and lived in boxcars or tents, then in section houses that the railroad provided. They finally bought homes and vacated the section houses in the 1950s.

But this chapter is not just about who lived where, in what type of architecture, and when their house was built. It is also about sitting on the front porch and waiting for the school bell to ring.

The William R. Rich family lived in this house at 213 Pine Street. Rich's brother-in-law C.K. Schantz built it using the same plans he had used for his own home in Iowa. The house is now in the McKinley Residential Historic District, named for McKinley School. (Courtesy Zona Galle.)

John Russell, his wife, and
children are arranged in a typical
family portrait pose in the mid-
1890s. Russell and a business
partner, Edd Stellers, operated
a meat market on Main Street.
(Courtesy Thelma Weston Estate.)

A view of Southwest Third Street
from about 1910 shows the tower
of Zion Lutheran Church on the
corner of Poplar Street. Like any
city, Newton has lost many of its
older houses, but Third Street is
one of several streets where homes
constructed during two building
booms, the 1880s and the years
around 1910, are still inhabited.
(Courtesy Zion Lutheran Church.)

John Jacob Krehbiel and his wife, Anna, commemorate their 50th wedding anniversary. Krehbiel learned his trades, blacksmithing and wagon making, during the Civil War. He moved his family to Newton from Iowa in 1879 and opened a blacksmith shop, which became Newton Carriage Works. Krehbiel also became cofounder of Bethel College and an important donor to Bethel Deaconess Hospital. He helped organize Mennonite Mutual Fire Insurance Company. The park beside the old carriage factory building is named John Jacob Krehbiel Memorial Park, and the iron fence surrounding it once surrounded Krehbiel's home. (Courtesy Carriage Factory Art Gallery.)

Descendants of John Jacob and Anna Krehbiel gather for a family portrait, probably as part of the couple's 50th wedding anniversary celebration. The Krehbiels had seven children. The couple is in the third row, fourth and fifth from the left. After he turned his factory over to his eldest son in the early 1900s, John Jacob and his wife traveled. He died at 83 years of age in 1921. Anna died in 1923. Both are buried in Greenwood Cemetery. (Courtesy Carriage Factory Art Gallery.)

This view of the 300 block of East Fourth Street shows some variety in architecture, but a preference for front porches prevails. The homes are now part of the McKinley Residential Historic District, and most were built between 1885 and 1920. They include the home of Jerry and Karen Wall. The Wall home once belonged to one of Newton's first optometrists, Dr. M.L. "Mordie" Woods, who moved to Newton around 1910. Many of the trees along the street are gone, victims of Dutch Elm disease. (Courtesy Karen Wall.)

HIGH SCHOOL, NEWTON, KANSAS—6

Newton's first school was established in 1872, and the first Newton High School class graduated in 1884, with diplomas but no ceremony. The site of the oldest of the brick high school buildings constructed in Newton has become part of the recently expanded Santa Fe School campus. (Courtesy Loyette Polhans Olson and Beverley Buller.)

The Newton School System Board of Education in 1941 included, from left to right, Laura (Mrs. Walter) Ingold, J.E. Wallace, Clarence Goering, Art Darling, George Deschner, Leonard Nelson, Ross Overstreet, and Dorothy (Mrs. Walter) Trousdale. (Courtesy Diana Claassen.)

Early Newton schools, such as Ward 1 School, were named for neighborhoods, but were later given formal names. Presidents' names became popular, and included Lincoln School (shown here), Washington, McKinley, and Roosevelt. Cooper School was named for a longtime superintendent. Some present schools are named Santa Fe, Slate Creek, Southbreeze, Sunset, Northridge, and Chisholm, but Newton High School has always had the same name. (Courtesy Thelma Weston Estate.)

Six

FUN, GAMES, AND SOCIAL OCCASIONS

In the days before there were televisions to turn on or computer games to play, when visiting another town simply for amusement was logistically difficult, there were still ways to have fun: make a few plans, use one's imagination, or take the opportunity as it arose. Fun was often more social than today, involving groups of people rather than isolated individuals amusing themselves indoors.

Newton residents found many pastimes, ranging from organized celebrations to simpler fun, like fishing or boating at Sand Creek. The photographs in this chapter will show some of the enjoyment of a bygone era.

According to a 1922 edition of the *Newton Kansan*, by the time the town was 50 years old, there were numerous lodges, clubs, and social organizations. Many of these had a benevolent function in addition to providing social interaction for members.

Entertainment venues were established. As early as 1885, an opera house was built. Later, there was a municipal auditorium, parks, theaters, a public pool, a racetrack, and a bandstand. There have been community bands, theater groups, athletic clubs, choruses, and county fairs.

Having fun in Newton could be as simple as a picnic or as elaborate as a weeklong festival celebrating the heritage of the Chisholm Trail.

The Ragsdale Opera House, an opulent structure built for $800,000 by two brothers in 1885, thrived at first but eventually fell into decline, partially due to a general financial panic in the 1890s. On January 1, 1915, a couple walking home from a New Year's Eve party discovered the opera house on fire. It burned to the ground, but only one person was killed. (Courtesy Dr. Gil Michel.)

An artist's rendition shows features of the interior of the Ragsdale Opera House. Between its opening on December 8, 1885, and its destruction by fire on January 1, 1915, the opera house hosted 695 plays, 72 concerts, 38 operas, 26 animal acts, lecturers including Helen Keller, political campaigns, and former Newton resident and operatic tenor Orville Harold. The building had offices for rent downstairs, a meeting hall, and an upstairs performing arts center seating 840 people. Phil Anderson remembers that his grandfather had a concession business there. He still has a big wooden box from it, with "Ragsdale" and "P.M. Anderson" written on it. (Courtesy Todd Hanchett.)

A group of children pose at the cannon at Military Park on this souvenir postcard. Originally called East Park, Military Park was renamed on October 5, 1899. One of the best-known sights in the park today is a Baldwin locomotive engine on display. The cannon, commemorating the Civil War veterans who settled in Newton, is still there. The park was also once known for its tree-lined Lovers' Lane. (Courtesy Todd Hanchett.)

Bess Benn (center) and two friends get ready for a ride. Benn played piano for silent movies at the Regent Theatre, grew up to marry Art Darling, was employed by Santa Fe Railroad, and volunteered at the Newton USO. (Courtesy Diane Claassen.)

Newton High School basketball player Art Darling, holding gun and birds, shows off bounty from a day's hunt with friends. To Darling's left is his coach, Frank Lindley. Darling scored the winning basket in the 1916 Kansas State Championship game, the first of several state titles for Newton under Lindley's leadership. The two became lifelong friends. (Courtesy Diane Claassen.)

Spectators enjoy automobile racing at the local track, which is now a circular drive in Athletic Park along Sand Creek. Newspaper accounts referred to it as "the fastest half-mile in the state." The same track was used for horse racing and county fair events. The original owner was the Newton Driving & Athletic Club. Dr. John Thomas Axtell and a group of his associates bought the property and developed the track, grandstand, exhibition buildings, and stables. Later, they dammed Sand Creek to create a swimming, boating, and skating lake. Newton residents voted 248 to 122 in favor of a $5,000 bond issue for city purchase of the park in 1909. (Courtesy John Wiebe.)

Contestants in a barrel race down Sand Creek get a starting push from their partners. Bess Benn, second barrel rider from right, was afraid of water but her boyfriend Art Darling, behind her, talked her into the race anyway, her granddaughter Diane Claassen said. Bess placed second. The race is an example of inventive fun that people created back in "the good old days." (Courtesy Diane Claassen.)

Y. M. C. A. Building, Newton, Kansas.

This Young Men's Christian Association (YMCA) operated from about 1909 into the 1970s. Activities included basketball, volleyball, and swimming. Newton's first YMCA, organized about 1886, hosted lectures and religious meetings, and lasted about four years. Welsh Livery Stable on West Sixth Street housed the second Y during fundraising for a new building. YMCA, which offered rooms for rent in the 1920s, nearly closed in the 1930s before a local resident paid its debts. Room rentals ended in the 1940s. YMCA hosted basketball leagues, swimming, archery competitions, and parties. Activities moved into school gymnasiums as the facility aged, and in 1973, it was closed and given to the Newton Recreation Commission. A new city recreation center not affiliated with the YMCA was built. The YMCA building was demolished in 1975. (Courtesy John Wiebe.)

The Union of Machinists, Boiler Makers and Blacksmiths, Santa Fe, present their entry in the 1920 Labor Day Parade. F.W. Woolworth's, a photography studio, and Kopke Brothers Public Service Grocery Store were in the 600 block of Main Street. Railroad retiree Glenn Patrick remembers that his father, as a former railroad employee, considered going back to his original trade, masonry, during a strike in the 1920s. The elder Patrick said that unions began in the 1930s and helped improve wages and work conditions. (Courtesy Phil Anderson.)

Newton residents enjoyed parades and held contests for the best-decorated float or vehicle. This one, entered by the Business and Professional Women's Club, won two prizes of $25 each in October 1928. The prizes did not quite pay for the float, designed by J.M. Supernois, a professional window dresser, because it cost them $61.75 to make it. The women riding the float include Elornia Getz, Vivian Tennie, Lowis Lowellen, and Elizabeth Clabough. (Courtesy Monica Supernois.)

Art Darling (first row, left) was player/coach in 1921 when Newton Athletic Club won the Kansas and Oklahoma basketball championship. The athletic club allowed young men who had already finished school a way to continue enjoying team sports. (Courtesy Diane Claassen.)

The 4-C Cabin Camp was located northeast of Newton, where old Highway 50 intersected Logan Street. John E. Wiebe (left) holds the horse, while Warren Riley (center) sits on the buggy with two unidentified riders. The man at far right is Harry Riley, who owned and operated the camp. John Wiebe remembers that this photograph was taken in the early 1930s. (Courtesy John Wiebe.)

Train themes have remained popular in Newton for all of the town's history, and parade floats are no exception. This miniature streamliner-style Santa Fe engine was featured in a 1947 Labor Day parade through downtown. Some of the spectators found a high vantage point in the second story of Superior Food Market. (Photograph by Frank Little Jr.; courtesy Patti Little Hollingshead.)

Back in 1943, when children used their imaginations while playing, these boys took their homemade wooden guns to Sand Creek for some fun based on gangster movies. Years later, after finding this photograph, taken in front of a West Broadway home, Jerry Jacobson named the group the Sand Creek Gang. Shown here are, from left to right, Chester ("Chet") Hartman, Jerry Jacobson, Frank Jones, Arlen Anderson, Joe Jones, Bobbie Minick, and Loren Anderson. Chet Hartman was the only boy wearing shoes that day. (Courtesy Jerry Jacobson.)

This ticket admitted the bearer to a New Year's Eve jamboree presented by the Regent Theatre in 1945. The Regent opened in 1907, so it was already operating when "talkies," or movies with sound, replaced silent films in the 1920s. (Courtesy Loyette Polhans Olson and Beverley Buller.)

Diane Darling, Newton High School's 1950 Homecoming Queen (left), attends festivities with classmates Jim Shepler (second from left), Irene Fotopoulos (third from left), and Bob Bocock. Darling remembers that Fotopoulos's father operated the Sunflower Café in downtown Newton. The high school team is still called the Railers in honor of the Santa Fe Railroad. (Courtesy Diane Claassen.)

NEWTON, KS - JULY 3, 4, 5, 1998

GRAND SLAM!

50th ANNUAL

"The Oldest Mexican-American Men's
Fastpitch Softball Tournament in the Country"

In 1946, Newton began hosting the Mexican-American Men's Fastpitch Softball Tournament. This Fourth of July weekend tradition is the oldest of four such tournaments in the country and takes place in Athletic Park. The program shown here commemorates the tournament's 50th anniversary. Softball has been a fixture in the Newton Mexican American community for decades. The first tournaments began in the 1930s, and companies like the Santa Fe Railroad would set aside practice time for teams. One early team, called the Cuauhtemoc, bought its uniforms from Anderson's for $27. The store allowed the team to pay on credit. The Cuauhtemoc became the local champions of 1932. In 1947, women's games were added between men's games to give male players a rest break. Starting in 1948, the tournament became a fundraiser for Our Lady of Guadalupe Church. Eventually, the church built its own ballpark. (Courtesy Albert Monares.)

Frank Lindley coached from 1914 to 1945 and was Newton High School's principal from 1921 to 1951. His record includes 18 Ark Valley championships, nine state championships, and eight league and seven state runner-up finishes. Called the "Father of Railer Basketball," Lindley received numerous honors and had a gymnasium named for him while he was still coaching. He invented zone defense. (Courtesy Phil Anderson.)

Newton won the 1936 state championship title in basketball, continuing a dynasty that Coach Lindley began two decades earlier. On the winning team that year were, from left to right, (first row) Coach Frank Lindley, Earl Oakes, Harry Bafus, Bill Ravenscroft, Leason "Pete" McCloud, Sid Holbert, and Coach Harold Hunt; (second row) Wilbur Flottmam, Gene Miller, Rex Neubauer, Paul Schmidt, Gene Grove, Delbert McDonnough, Lloyd Phillips, and Coach John Ravenscroft. The team had a 22-2 record that year. (Courtesy Phil Anderson.)

FRANK L. LINDLEY
Principal

Artist Lawrence Davenport painted several Newton landmarks, including Lindley Hall. The gymnasium at the corner of Seventh and Poplar Streets was built in 1934 and named for Frank Lindley, Newton's head basketball coach and high school principal. Newton High won championships in Lindley Hall from 1935 to 1973. The gym has been featured in books and a film, *Hallowed Hardwood: Vintage Basketball Gyms of Kansas*. (Courtesy Phil Anderson.)

In 1951, The Newton Railers returned to the state high school basketball finals. The team surrounds Coach John Ravenscroft during a time-out. Clockwise from lower left are Larry Davenport, Clarence Waters, Ken Schlup, Jim Tangeman, Ravenscroft, Gene Smith (partially hidden), and manager Phil Anderson. On the bench are, from left to right, Eldon Akers, Ken Kennard, Bill Brainard, Don Quiring, Marlo Reimer, and Coach Curtis Fisher. Ravenscroft played at Newton, then assisted Coach Frank Lindley on his 1936 state championship team before playing at the University of Colorado. In 13 years at Newton, he led the Railers to four state championships, 11 Ark Valley championships, and four state second-place showings. (Courtesy Phil Anderson.)

Sisters Normadeen and Neva Luttrell wait in front of the roller-skating rink for their friends to join them on a Saturday afternoon in 1943. The Starlite Skating Rink closed in 2012, after operating in Newton since 1937. In 1963, when Sue and Doug Decker moved to Newton, the two children talked their parents, Van and Vera Decker, into buying the rink. The family sold it in 1987. (Courtesy Monica Supernois.)

With so many shops in downtown Newton, Christmas decorations were not confined to window displays. This one, featuring a painted Santa Claus and his reindeer among snow-covered Christmas trees, was mounted above a furniture store in 1955. The display was made by Calvin Supernois. (Courtesy Monica Supernois.)

This parade float celebrates Newton's photographers. Several notable studios in Newton's history included Tripp Photography, W.R. Murphy, McDaniel Photography Studio, and H.S. Stovall (who called himself "The Panorama Man"). A developer's stamp on this photograph indicates that it was taken during Newton's 75th anniversary parade. Parades used to be held in Newton on Booster's Day and Labor Day, two occasions no longer celebrated. In 1971, the Newton centennial celebration included a parade. More recently, processions down Main Street celebrate the annual Chisholm Trail Festival and Christmas. Here, the float is passing the J.S. Dillons & Sons store, which was a grocery. The original Newton store, sixth in a chain, opened in 1929. The franchise continued to expand, and Newton now has two Dillons stores. (Courtesy Bethany Mace and Rosie Wiebe.)

An antique hearse, complete with drivers in top hats and fringed harness for the horses, participates in Newton's 75th anniversary parade. The hearse passing a car dealership makes an interesting contrast between past and present. Several other photographs from this parade also featured historic themes. (Courtesy Brad Anderson.)

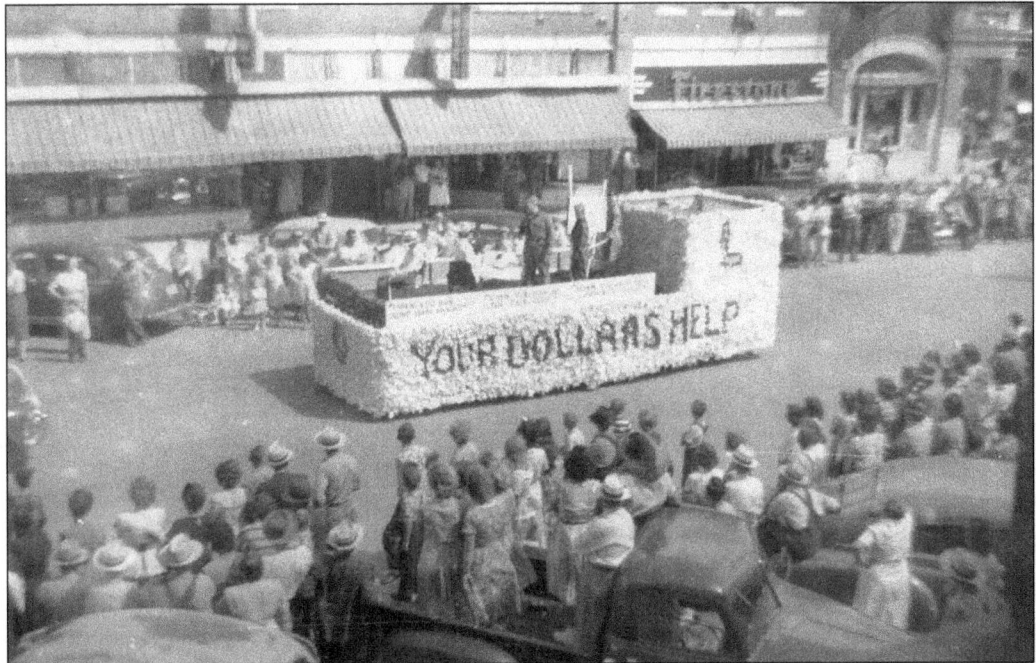

This Lion's Club float promoting charitable giving passes the local Firestone dealership. Newton has been home to a number of lodges and benevolent organizations in its history. The Masonic lodge was among the first. The lodge building still houses offices facing Main Street, with the Masonic part of the building facing the side. The building even housed county offices before construction of the old Harvey County Courthouse. (Courtesy Brad Anderson.)

A wedding is always a memorable social occasion. Here, on their November 4, 1945, wedding day are bride Grace Bestvater Kasitz and groom Harry Kasitz. The wedding was celebrated at Newton Evangelical and Reformed Church. The couple's car was decorated so that everyone would know about the newlyweds. (Courtesy Harry Kasitz.)

The Newton Swimming Pool in Athletic Park opened in the late 1930s, replacing a lake created by damming Sand Creek. Zona Galle, whose mother, Selma, served on a committee to help desegregate the pool and local theaters, said the pool was originally for whites only. African Americans could swim there only one day each year, just before the pool was drained at the end of the season. (Courtesy Bethany Mace and Rosie Wiebe.)

Newton Community Theater was established in 1965 by Arlo Kasper, Sam Nance, and Helen Canzoneri. In nearly 50 years, the group has performed more than 100 shows, including melodramas for the annual Chisholm Trail Festival. Here, founder Arlo Kasper (left) performs comedy with Jack Frey. (Courtesy Sharon Koehn and Arlo Kasper.)

Until Newton Library was built in the 1970s, Military Park had a bandstand. Santa Fe retiree Charlie Smith sang there with a vocal group, Charles Charles and the Falling Stars, in the late 1960s and early 1970s. From left to right are Albert Martinez, Robert Martinez, and Smith. The group traveled and charged for shows at clubs and similar venues, but performed gospel music for free, "just for the joy of it," Smith said. They performed all over Kansas and Oklahoma. (Courtesy Charlie Smith.)

The Bethel College Mennonite Church quilting group combines social time with work. The church has had an active quilting group for many years. The finished quilts benefit missions and relief efforts. (Courtesy Bethel College Mennonite Church.)

Harry Kasitz drives a team of oxen during a parade. He drove this team, which he trained, in various parades including some in Newton. Work required him to move away from Newton for many years, but he often returned for celebrations and eventually became a Newton resident again. (Courtesy Harry Kasitz.)

104

Six

NEWTON AT WORSHIP

Newton has always been, as the 50th anniversary edition of the *Newton Kansan* put it in 1922, "a city of churches." Many local houses of worship are nearly as old as the town.

To people arriving in a new place, religious faith was both important and comfortingly familiar. Immigrants brought their particular religious denominations with them from their native countries. The Mennonite farmers are most often mentioned, but other groups came, too. Mexicans, Greeks, Italians, Irish, and African Americans most often came to work for the railroad.

New arrivals congregated anywhere they could, including private homes, rented buildings, churches of other denominations, tents, railcars, basements, and even a skating rink. Early stories of Newton often refer to religion. One tale describes a fellow who took his message where he thought sinners were likely to hear it; he preached in the Gold Room Saloon, and was rewarded for his efforts with a donation of money and a social drink.

Churches have always provided important socialization. Each congregation has groups within it, whether they are choirs, women's or men's organizations, Sunday schools, youth clubs, mission groups, disaster-response teams, or sponsored activities like scout troops. They are, essentially, extended families.

The number of churches in Newton often changes. This chapter can include only a sampling, because new ones constantly join the list. Some congregations have been firmly established in the same spot for more than a century. Others, like families growing out of starter homes, have changed addresses several times. A few, like the ones advertising in Spanish, have arisen from a need to serve a particular segment of the community. Others are part of an interdenominational trend.

The presence of so many houses of worship reminds people in Newton that one of the town's foundations is, and always has been, faith in God.

First Methodist Church members gather for a photograph in front of the building they used from the 1880s through 1917. This church, on Seventh and Main Streets, was the second home for the congregation, which was established in 1873. Now called First United Methodist Church, the congregation built a new home on the same site, and it still stands there today. It is also the parent church of Trinity and East Side United Methodist churches. (Courtesy First United Methodist Church.)

St. Matthew's Episcopal Church dates back to 1876. Its present building, on Windsor Drive, was constructed in 1958. The congregation met in various buildings until finding its first home in a stone building that no longer exists. The second building, on Broadway, was purchased from a Methodist congregation that had built a new church. (Courtesy Loyette Polhans Olson and Beverley Buller.)

Members of First Baptist Church of Newton built the 1877 Meeting House at 210 West Fifth Street themselves without drawing up plans first. Their dedication ceremony on January 27, 1878, was followed by a weeklong revival and the baptism of 12 people in the cold waters of Sand Creek. In 1884, the Baptists moved and a succession of eight congregations, including Mennonites, German Baptists, Disciples of Christ, Evangelical Christians, Seventh-Day Adventists, and African American Methodists either owned or rented the meetinghouse. In 1968, when the African American Methodist Holsey Chapel faded out and an automobile dealership bought the property, the church seemed destined for demolition until Vern Bender, pastor of People's Bible Baptist Church, purchased the building and relocated it to the corner of East Twelfth and Logan Streets. (Courtesy First Baptist Church.)

First Baptist Church first met in the 1877 Meeting House and then bounced around several locations, including the Methodist church on Broadway and Poplar Streets and Eagle Hall Skating Rink on the corner of Plum and Sixth Streets. In 1884, the new church on Sixth and Poplar Streets was built at a cost of $12,000. Clara Auld donated a bell for the tower. (Courtesy First Baptist Church.)

First Church of the Nazarene in Newton celebrated its 100th anniversary in 2010. The congregation originally met in a residence, but in 1916, it purchased the old Newton Christian Church at Main and First Streets, shown here, and moved it to 1000 Main, where the brick church stands today. (Courtesy First Church of the Nazarene.)

Church of the Nazarene was a new denomination in the early 1900s when Newton was chosen to host the Second Annual District Assembly of the Church of the Nazarene. Presiding over the assembly were Dr. P.F. Bresee and his wife, both shown in this photograph. (Courtesy Newton First Church of the Nazarene.)

First United Church of Christ was the first merged congregation of the denomination that combined two older churches, Immanuel Evangelical and Reformed Church, and First Congregational Church. The First United Church of Christ building originally belonged to First Congregational Church, but the 1886 building was extensively rebuilt in 1909 and has been renovated several times since to retain the best features of each version. There is a bell tower, but no bell. Local legend says that, in 1886, a neighbor, not a member of the church, agreed to donate $50 to keep a bell from being installed because he did not want his sleep interrupted. (Courtesy United Church of Christ.)

The pipe organ in the First United Church of Christ is an example of how churches in Newton share facilities and resources. When the church replaced its pipe organ, it sold the original pipes to another church in town. When Immanuel Evangelical and Reformed Church merged with First Congregational Church to created First United Church of Christ, the Evangelical and Reform building at Seventh and Plum Streets was sold. (Courtesy First United Church of Christ.)

First Mennonite Church on First Street was organized in 1878 and got its first home in 1881. After enlarging the original building in 1902, the congregation raised enough money in 1930 to build a new church. Much of the labor was donated by church members. Many of the original families who settled in Newton have descendants who are members of First Mennonite Church. (Photograph by Robert Wiebe; courtesy Bethany Mace and Rosie Wiebe.)

BIRDS EYE VIEW NEWTON KANS.

The bird's-eye view was a popular genre of postcard in the early 1900s. Featured here are St. Mary's Catholic Church and several businesses, including C.H. Northfoss Furniture, Carpet and Undertaking at 716 North Main, in the foreground. Continuing north on Main Street, one would pass Newton Cornice Works, Fred Wing Bicycles, First Presbyterian Church, and the Harvey County Courthouse before arriving at St. Mary's. The congregation was started by four families meeting in tents and railcars in 1871. Their first building was completed in 1874 in the second block of Main, on the north side of East Sixth. A school soon followed. The arrival of a new pastor in 1900 led to construction of new church, school, and parish buildings between Main and Oak on Eighth Street, and by 1922, the property covered half the block and the church had more than 500 members, plus an active Knights of Columbus chapter and Ladies Altar Society. St. Mary's Church and school are still there today. In 1920, St. Mary's built a chapel near the largest Mexican Camp on West First Street, then expanded it the following year. This chapel became the first home of Our Lady of Guadalupe Catholic Church. The present home of Our Lady of Guadalupe was built on South Ash Street after members started a fundraising drive for the new building in 1958. (Courtesy Karen Jacobson.)

First Presbyterian Church, showcased on this 1908 postcard, was one of the first churches in Newton, organized on July 7, 1872. Harmony Presbyterian Church of Pittsburgh, Pennsylvania, took up a collection and donated the first $15 toward construction of the Newton church on West Sixth Street. Later, the building was moved and incorporated into a larger church at Main and Seventh Streets, which was completed in 1904 and dedicated the following year. (Courtesy Todd Hanchett.)

First Christian Church, Newton, Kansas

First Christian Church met in this white wooden church, seen here on a postcard along with part of East First Street, until moving to Ninth and Main Streets. Later, the church returned to 102 East First, and now meets in a modern brick building. (Courtesy John Wiebe.)

Old Baptist Church, just before the new one was built.

The bell tower had been removed when the congregation of First Baptist Church met for the last time at their old church on Sixth and Poplar Streets. Construction of the new church started on the same site in 1923. The first service was in April 1926, and the dedication followed on June 19, 1927. The first baptism in the new building was of the pastor's son, Joyce Hardy. (Courtesy First Baptist Church.)

Zion Lutheran Evangelical Church first met in private homes with a visiting pastor. It was formally organized in 1886 by German immigrants who came to Newton on the Santa Fe Railroad to buy land offered at "reasonable prices." They built this church on the corner of Southwest Third and Poplar Streets later that same year and also used it for a school. This class photograph from 1888 includes 23 boys, 17 girls, and 5 adults. School met there until 1947. (Courtesy Zion Lutheran Church.)

This Church was dedicated Aug. 9, 1903. Mr. August Anders was the builder. Pastor J.W. Dukewitz served us at that time.

The second Zion Lutheran Church, featuring a tower and Gothic windows, was dedicated on August 9, 1903. That building became part of the present-day brick church, dedicated in 1929. Additions include an education wing built in 1955 and a new sanctuary in 1966. Zion Lutheran's 100th anniversary was celebrated in March 1986. (Courtesy Zion Lutheran Church.)

Zion Lutheran Church added an education wing in 1955. The taller part of the church incorporates the second church building, which was originally a wooden structure. Part of the old building's roofline can still be seen, revealing where the newer building begins. (Courtesy Zion Lutheran Church.)

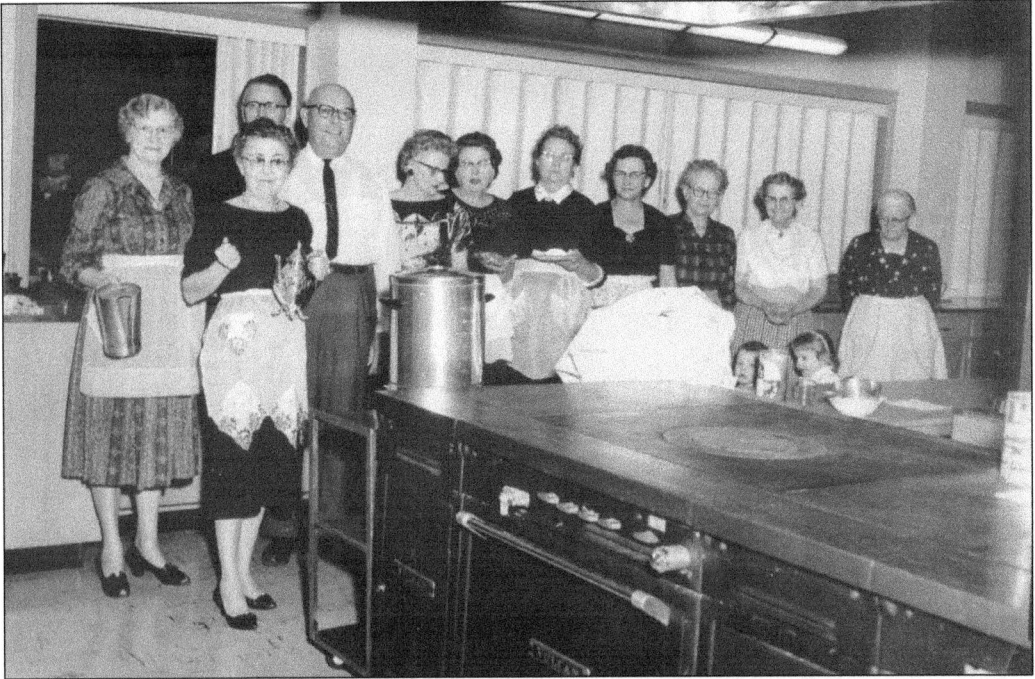

When Bethel College Mennonite Church constructed a new building in 1956, the kitchen was the first room completed. Gathered on January 30, 1960, to prepare the food for the wedding reception for Susan Schmidt and Keith Rhoades are, from left to right, Anna Siemens, Ann Goering, Otto Warkentin, August Epp, Lena Warkentin, Esther Schmidt, Elizabeth Loewen, Helen Epp, Anna Unruh, Emelia Bartel, and Sarah Unruh. The children with them are David and Lori Ensz. (Courtesy Bethel College Mennonite Church.)

Newton Bible Church met in a basement for four years while its congregation raised money to build a sanctuary. Church member Michael Kelton remembers a story from the early 1950s about a prospective pastor who asked a gas station attendant where Newton Bible Church was. The attendant said, "Oh, you mean the groundhog church?" The church members built a home on Old Main Street and dedicated it in 1960. Here, Pastor Jim Conway waves from the top of the framework in 1959. Matt Kruse is currently pastor. (Courtesy Newton Bible Church.)

This photograph was taken at a service inside Newton Bible Church, probably during the 1960s. Bethany Mace remembers when her grandparents, Rosie and Robert Wiebe, told her about being among the founding members of the church when it was started in the 1950s. (Courtesy Bethany Mace and Rosie Wiebe.)

In 1971, Newton Bible Church dedicated a new Sunday school addition to its building at 900 Old Main Street. A second addition expanded the church in 1994, and a gymnasium was added in 1997. The church opened Newton Bible Christian School at the same location in 1973. (Courtesy Newton Bible Church.)

East Side United Methodist Church passed the half-century mark in 2011. One of the features of its services in recent years has been bluegrass Sundays. Band members have varied, but among those participating have included, shown here from left to right, Marge Barnard, Vic Barnard, John Lenke, Jan Schroeder, and Vern Schroeder. (Courtesy East Side United Methodist Church.)

Immanuel Baptist Mission became Immanuel Baptist Church in 1974. Here, members commemorate their first meeting with a photograph in front of the Leon Blackwell home on October 3, 1965. Later, the congregation met at Sister Frieda Chapel for several years before constructing its own building on North Anderson Road in 1975. The church was dedicated in September 1977. (Courtesy Immanuel Baptist Church.)

Sister Frieda Chapel served as the second home of Immanuel Baptist Church. The congregation met there for the first time in December 1965. The chapel originally served the Deaconess organization and Bethel Hospital and is named for Sr. Frieda Kaufman, a Mennonite deaconess who was first superintendent of Bethel Deaconess Hospital. (Courtesy Immanuel Baptist Church.)

120

Members and guests of Immanuel Baptist Church get together for a fellowship meal in the basement of Sister Frieda Chapel in the early 1970s. Fellowship meals continue to be a tradition at this church and many others. (Courtesy Immanuel Baptist Church.)

On March 11, 1962, an addition was added to the first building.

Koerner Heights Church started on May 4, 1958, meeting in Newton City Auditorium. It dedicated its first building exactly one year later. The congregation also helped start Hesston Mennonite Brethren Church and Halstead Community Bible Church of Mennonite Brethren and continues its mission projects. (Courtesy Koerner Heights Church.)

The congregation of Shalom Mennonite Church was formally organized in 1988 and met for a while in Sister Frieda Chapel. The church then purchased and moved into the former Bible Baptist Church building, which is seen here from the air. (Courtesy Shalom Mennonite Church.)

Grace Community Church members attend a worship service. The church was dedicated on November 24, 1991. David Reimer served as its first pastor. The church has grown enough for several expansions and has added a playground for the younger members of the congregation. (Courtesy Grace Community Church.)

Seven

NORTH NEWTON

North Newton, originally part of Newton, was incorporated on September 20, 1938. North Newton's most prominent feature is Bethel College.

When Bethel College was founded in 1887, little more than farmland surrounded it. The section around the school eventually started resembling a town, but farmland still separated Newton and North Newton when the towns divided in 1938. There are mostly houses between them now.

Stories about why the towns split have circulated for years. A 125th-anniversary edition of the *Newton Kansan*, published on August 21, 1997, explained one that is often heard: the predominantly Mennonite North Newton residents faced persecution during World War I because they were pacifists of German descent, and anything German was suspect.

That tale has been discounted based on the number of years between the end of the war and when the division actually occurred, although vandalism in North Newton was blamed on some Newton residents when World War II brought back anti-German sentiment. Actually, North Newton needed to incorporate to get New Deal funding for a sewer system. The City of Newton agreed, wanting to avoid possible pollution in Sand Creek from existing septic tanks. And, of course, local residents say North Newton has always centered around the college.

The story of how North Newton got its name is all about the US Postal Service. Newton had its post office, but North Newton had a separate one to serve Bethel College. Post office names did not always match town names, especially when there was more than one. The post office at the college, Bethel College Post Office, caused confusion because Kansas has a town called Bethel. The post office ordered a name change, and North Newton was chosen. When the new town incorporated, it used the post office name.

The two city governments are separate, but some services and organizations, like the Newton/ North Newton Historic Preservation Commission, water, and fire protection are shared between these neighbors with similar names.

The first building constructed at Bethel College now serves as the administration building. The college was created through a private corporation formed in 1887 by prominent Newtonians David Goertz, Bernhard Warkentin, J.J. Krehbiel, Arthur B. Gilbert, Charles R. McLain, and James M. Ragsdale. A charter was received later that year, and the cornerstone was laid on October 12, 1888. Construction on the limestone building was delayed several years by slow fundraising, but was finally finished in 1893. A dedication ceremony followed on September 19, and school started the next day, with five teachers and 98 students. There were about 10 buildings on campus when the first class graduated in 1912. (Courtesy Todd Hanchett.)

SCIENCE HALL, BETHEL COLLEGE,
NORTH NEWTON, KANSAS

Another prominent building constructed at Bethel College was Science Hall, added in 1925 and joining Alumni Hall, Carnegie Hall, and others. Like many other buildings on campus, the Science Hall cornerstone was laid on the same day of the year as the original building, October 12. The building has been renovated into an academic building. In 2012, Bethel College, which is the oldest Mennonite college in the United States, celebrated its 125th anniversary during the school's annual Fall Festival. (Courtesy Loyette Polhans Olsen and Beverley Buller.)

Kauffman Museum, across from Bethel College, started when Charles Kauffman moved his collection from Freeman, South Dakota, to North Newton in 1940. Today, the museum emphasizes the history of Mennonite migration into America, particularly Kansas, and prairie life. Among the buildings is the Voth-Unruh-Fast House, named for three families who lived there. The 19th-century farmhouse was moved to the museum grounds from east of Goessel in 1973. Nearby is the 1886 Ratzlaff Barn. The grounds also feature a prairie reconstruction of native plant life. (Courtesy Harvey County Historical Museum and Archive.)

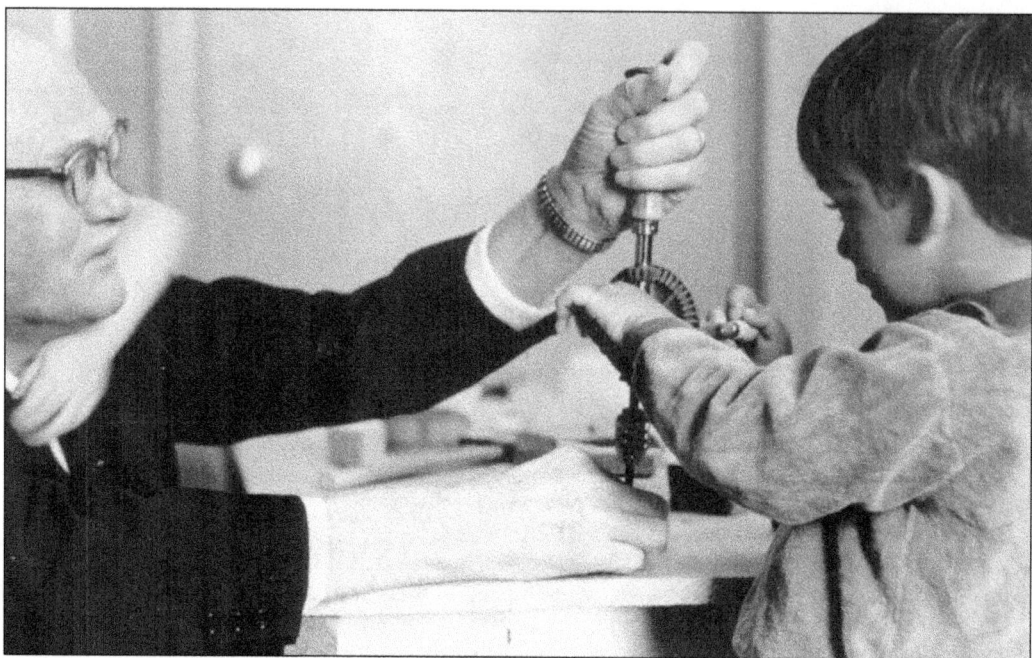

Helping to get the younger generation off to a good start is the Community Play School, hosted by Bethel College Mennonite Church. Here, "Grandpa" Unruh shows one of the children how to operate an old-fashioned hand drill as he teaches them about carpentry work. (Courtesy Bethel College Mennonite Church.)

Two children at the Community Play School at Bethel College Mennonite Church concentrate on their activities while adults offer supervision and encouragement. These youngsters were part of the 1984–1985 class. The play school is open to the general public and continues to serve local children. (Courtesy Bethel College Mennonite Church.)

Passengers at Newton's train station wait to board Amtrak Train No. 3, also known as the Southwest Chief, shortly before 3:00 a.m. The train, one of the last passenger trains stopping in Newton, runs between Chicago and Los Angeles. The only other passenger train making the Newton stop, Amtrak Train No. 4, runs the same route in the opposite direction and is scheduled to arrive each night a few minutes after Train No. 3. On this particular night, the train had only two coaches. At the time of this book's publication, rerouting is being considered that would turn the train at Newton and send it through part of Oklahoma and into Texas, ending a tradition of passenger service in western Kansas. While the authors feel it is appropriate to end a book about Newton with a railroad photo, they hope the tradition of passenger service through Newton will not end any time soon. (Photograph by Dena Bisnette.)

Visit us at
arcadiapublishing.com